D1453547

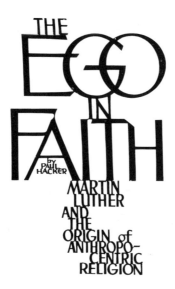

THE EGO IN FAITH

by PAUL HACKER

MARTIN LUTHER AND THE ORIGIN of ANTHROPO-CENTRIC RELIGION

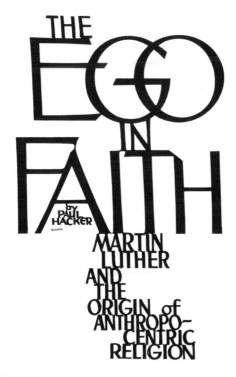

THE EGO IN FAITH

BY PAUL HACKER

MARTIN LUTHER AND THE ORIGIN of ANTHROPO-CENTRIC RELIGION

FRANCISCAN HERALD PRESS

THE EGO IN FAITH, by Paul Hacker, is a condensed recast by the author of his work, *Das Ich im Glauben bei Martin Luther,* published by Styria Verlag, Graz (Austria), 1966. Library of Congress Catalog Card Number: 70-85506, ISBN 8199 0406-6. Copyright 1970 by Franciscan Herald Press, 1434 West 51st Street, Chicago, Illinois 60609. Made in the United States of America.

###

NIHIL OBSTAT:
  Mark Hegener O.F.M.
  Censor Deputatus

IMPRIMATUR:
  Rt. Rev. Msgr. Francis W. Byrne
  Vicar General, Archdiocese of Chicago

October 4, 1970

Preface

At first sight this book seems to be contrary to the prevailing atmosphere of irenic dialogue between various religious denominations. The fact is that today both sides of the two faiths (Catholic and Lutheran) to a great extent regard it as necessary to speak of Luther only in terms of praise. But does the effort to understand one another exclude a critical study if the cause of truth is served in this way? Is it not true that, besides the known differences in the tenets of the Catholic and Lutheran religions, there is a basis of differences even in the writings of Luther himself? Perhaps there are mental presuppositions which stand in the way of a mutual understanding, because they are so much a part of the Lutheran's way of thinking that he hardly ever gives expression to them, while for the Catholic they are so strange that he cannot easily detect them.

This book is the result of studies on Luther which were carried on over a period of years. The author began with the sincere determination that if he discovered certain points in Luther's doctrine he would honestly criticize and reject them. He felt that it was above all the concept of faith, developed by Luther since the end of 1517, which was the essential and spiritual cause of the great split in the religion of western Christendom. In fact, this concept introduced a "new theology," concerning

which Cajetan in one of his writings of 1518 remarked prophetic-
ally: "This means nothing less than the founding of a new
church."

This new idea of faith, conflicting with the opposite notion,
brought about a total change in Luther's spiritual life and thought.
It was the real reason for his opposition to the Roman Church.
It may have been the driving force which, instead of leading to
a reform of the one Church, led to a breaking away from it and
then to ever-widening separatist movements. In ever-widening
circles, it influenced not only the theology but also the spiritual
history of modern times.

The present book examines the nature of this concept of faith,
its development, and its effects on Luther's spiritual life and thinking. As stated, this book is a critical investigation. Again and
again it allows Luther to speak for himself and it takes him at
his word. To the author this critical attitude was of great personal
significance; but for others too, his book will not have been
written in vain if it makes them think over the question of the
Reformation and Protestantism and the relation between true reform and the unity of the Church. It contains essential elements
which can and must be utilized with fruit in the present-day
tasks of the Church and Ecumenism.

To one who peruses this book in a superficial way, it may seem
to be at first sight like an anachronism. . . . Naturally it has its
limitations, as the author himself confesses. It cannot aim to
portray the entire Luther. Although it regards it as necessary to
point out that in the heart of Luther's work there is a turning
away from the center of the Gospel, it does not for an instant
question the fact that from Luther's work, especially his sermons,
there goes forth a positive Christian challenge. . . . This is not a
book which aims to set up a tribunal guided by a preconceived
definite stand. On the contrary, it presents an open-minded in-
terchange with Luther concerning the truth of the Gospel. This
alone is what counts. . . . In one respect, it is not a "modern"
book — namely in the definite way in which it takes up the
question of the truth, that is the real meaning of the Gospel, and
then enters upon a dialogue with historical facts. . . . It must be
conceded that here and there something like an "Ecumenism of

Resignation" has come into vogue, an ecumenism which considers it old-fashioned to carry on any kind of debate for the purpose of arriving at the truth. However, from such an ecumenism Christianity can hope to arrive at nothing. It would spell its termination, because a peace which rests on a surrender of truth would be the equivalent of burying the faith. . . . This book seeks to pull people out of their neutral attitude and to make them ask questions together with the author. He has the right, therefore, to expect his work to be evaluated by the single norm he had in mind: the quest of the truth of the Gospel, whether it is pleasant or not, whether it coincides with one's ideas or makes them questionable. In this sense, I gladly endorse this work.

— JOSEPH RATZINGER

Contents

Introduction

Ecumenism is open to two kinds of misunderstanding or abuse. First, it can be misconceived as aiming merely at a *modus vivendi* and more friendly relations among communities that remain divided. Second, there seems to be a temptation for Catholics to represent Protestant views, formerly rejected by the Church, as not irreconcilable with Catholicism, to thin down Catholic doctrine to aspects that may be compatible with Protestant positions, and to dodge the differentiation between truth and error.

The Second Vatican Council, however, in welcoming the Ecumenical Movement and encouraging its progress, has not sanctioned such confusions. The Decree on Ecumenism repeatedly states that the aim of ecumenism is the restoration of full unity between the now divided communities (see nos. 1, 4, 5, 12). It is with this objective in view that the document readily admits that we can learn from the separated Christians (nos. 4, 6), and it urges that we should try to understand better the mind of the separated brethren (no. 9). But the Decree also demands "that it should become clearer what the position of the Catholic Church really is" and "that our faith be more adequately expounded" to the separated Christians (nos. 9, 11 para. 2). It warns that those things which we can learn from the separated Christians "have carefully to be distinguished from the Deposit of Faith" (no. 6). There is no room for a license to blur essential differences. The Decree explicitly cautions against confusion in stating: "Nothing is so alien to ecumenism as that false irenicism by which the purity of Catholic doctrine suffers damage and its genuine and plain sense is obscured" (*Nil ab oecumenismo tam alienum est quam ille falsus irenismus, quo puritas doctrinae catholicae detrimentum patitur et ejus sensus genuinus et certus obscuratur.* No. 11).

True ecumenism is a common quest for the truth and for possibilities of reëstablishing real unity. The principal objective of such endeavors is, of course, the discovery of agreements and a rapprochement without detriment to the truth. But since truth is opposed to error, it is also necessary to make distinctions and even to venture criticism. Honest inquiry for the truth does not evade the challenge of serious criticism.

Catholics are at present criticizing their own past and the present condition of their Church with a zeal which to some extent is surely justified and healthy, though it often overshoots the mark. But is it only Catholicism that requires to be criticized? Is it not necessary that the principles underlying the separate existence of Protestant Churches should also be critically examined?

The movement that resulted in the division was started by Martin Luther. Crucial to his theology and spirituality from about 1518 onward was his new conception of faith. This concept was a seed whose germinative power has remained unimpaired throughout four and a half centuries. It is the inchoate form of anthropocentric theology. Now it is anthropocentric trends which at present are causing considerable confusion in Protestantism and Catholicism alike, and the writings of modern Protestants evidence the impact of Luther's central idea. A critique of this idea seems therefore requisite for clarifying the situation.

But is it wise to reopen an old wound which has just begun to heal? Should we not be glad that the period dominated by controversy has at last come to an end? Would it not be more helpful to the cause of reconciliation to confine our studies to features in Luther's thought acceptable to all partners in the dialogue?

There is no one today who denies that there are genuinely Christian values in Luther's works. The present author is well aware that these can be made fruitful for true ecumenism and he has been anxious not to overlook such values even in writing this critique. However, experience of recent years has come to confirm his conviction that a positive evaluation of Luther's ideas presupposes criteria, and these can only be gained by critical scrutiny. The present confusion is in a great measure the outcome of a lack of criteria. Today, a critique of Luther's central concept is not a triumphant assertion of Catholic claims but an attempt to discern one of the origins of dangers that threaten all Churches alike.

The thought of pre-Protestant Luther (1509-17) is grand and deep. His passion for the Word of God, his "theology of the cross" and his spirituality of humility revivified vital elements of Catholic tradition with an originality indicative of charism. Even his anti-philosophical attitude is evidence of his total surrender to the majesty of God. His allegiance to nominalism did not impair his religious originality. On the contrary, he kept a critical attitude toward tenets of that school and succeeded in making its way of thinking subservient to his intention, which was exclusively and passionately religious. All the great impulses of a truly Christian nature that remained even in his later career date from that early period which, though very different from prevailing forms of medieval Catholicism, must be judged as the promise of a Catholic renewal.

But with the emergence of a new idea of the nature of faith a thorough mutation of Luther's theology and spirituality set in. The potential reformer became the first Protestant. The present book attempts to describe the new conception, to investigate its origin, to discuss the problem of its conformity with Holy Scripture, and to examine its implications for vital sections of Christian life. Thus we hope to find a criterion for a necessary discrimination. There are elements in Luther's thought that are consistent with the gospel and, accordingly, with Christian unity, and there are others which are not so. Only if we succeed in critically isolating the negative elements can we properly take up the positive suggestions.

Perhaps the venture of breaking the taboo of a criticism of Luther in our time can be undertaken only in the no-man's land between Protestantism and Catholicism. In fact it was there that the main outlines of what is here submitted to the reader's judgment were first drafted. The author began reading Luther many years ago as a Protestant with unreserved assent and in the conviction that the Reformer could help us find ways to unity. But his assent was vehemently shaken about ten years ago by a discovery which is described in the first section of this book. He then went on probing into Luther's writings. He noticed the difference between Luther's pre-Protestant and Protestant periods, the first extending to the end of 1517, the latter beginning from about 1520, with a transition period of some two years in between. The difference is marked by the rise and evolution of the new conception of faith.

The method followed in this book is first to allow Luther to speak himself. He is then taken at his word; that is to say, his words are taken actually to mean what they say in their respective contexts. The criterion by which his statements are judged is the one which he himself wished to see applied by anyone who might criticize him, in writing: "I beg, however, that he who wishes to go at me may equip himself with Scripture" (Weimar edition, vol. 6, p. 324). His original ideas are interpreted as the outcome of *experience*. It is true that these ideas belong in a historical context whose description can help us to "understand" them. But this kind of understanding would emphasize the distance between the one contemplating and the thing contemplated. Events seen in the context of past situations inevitably appear as more or less irrelevant to the present. However, what matters in Luther's thought is not so much its being *the result of past history* as the fact that it *resulted in making future history,* and this is the primary aspect from which the present author is viewing Luther's central idea. Only at one point of the investigation (Chapter V, Section 1) did it seem necessary to refer briefly to a historical situation of theological debate. However, this is only to set off Luther's originality against contemporary opinions. As for the rest, the author leaves to others the task — which is important and necessary — of clarifying the historical conditions in which Luther's ideas arose. My justification for this is, first, that my point of view may prove complementary to other methods.

Second, Luther himself time and again stressed the decisive importance of experience for his theology. Third, it is experience which forms the most original part of Luther's thought. Fourth, Luther's originality, grounded in experience, can alone account for the vitality of his influence throughout half a millennium. Therefore, attention to experience as a methodical and hermeneutic principle is dictated by the nature of Luther's thought.

The experience meant here is *spiritual* experience. Events of the spiritual life are not simply identical with psychic phenomena. It may even happen that spiritual experience runs contrary to psychic states. For instance, sublime spiritual joy can coexist with utter distress at the psychic level. Degraded spirituality, on the contrary, ends in psychic tangles. It is only in describing misdevelopments of spirituality that psychological interpretation seems in order.

Thus the clue proposed in the present book for an explanation of Luther's new conception of faith is neither dogmatics proper nor the history of dogma nor psychology nor external events, but the development, and misdevelopment, of Luther's spiritual life. The starting-point is, of course, doctrine that bears on the spiritual life. But in a man of Luther's caliber this has to be interpreted as expressive of his own spiritual personality.

The book is in the main a condensed recast in English of the author's German book *Das Ich im Glauben bei Martin Luther,* published by Styria Verlag, Graz (Austria), 1966. It does not render the German edition superfluous, since the latter includes some matter which is not incorporated in the American version. On the other hand, this recast points out aspects that had not yet been contemplated in the German book. Most of the matter has been thought over again and consequently reformulated and rearranged. In a few cases, the queries of reviewers have drawn the author's attention to fresh points of view. The introduction and several sections have been entirely rewritten.

The author acknowledges his indebtedness to Fr. Jared Wicks, S.J., and Fr. Otto H. Pesch, O.P., whose criticism stirred him to continue reflection or to clarify some points. Jared Wicks' book *Man Yearning for Grace — Luther's Early Spiritual Teaching* (Washington: Corpus Books, 1968) and the present book are complementary to, and slightly overlap, one another. While Fr. Wicks treats the spirituality Luther taught up to the rise of his new conception of faith, the present book singles out the spirituality — with emphasis on *lived* spirituality — of the Protestant Luther and describes the chief trait of this spirituality against the background of his early spiritual teaching.

The author wishes to tender his grateful thanks to an American theologian and friend who took the pains of atticizing his English *koiné*.

CHAPTER I

The New Conception of Faith

1. A Reinterpretation of the Creed

In Western Christendom, the content of faith has been summarized in the Apostles' Creed. Martin Luther expounded this Creed in his *Small Catechism,* which he published in 1529 and which became the most popular compendium of religious doctrine not only in Lutheranism but, in some groups, even beyond the limits of this denomination. An American version of Luther's exposition reads as follows:

The First Article. "I believe that God has made *me* and all creatures; that He has given *me my* body and soul, eyes, ears, and all *my* limbs, *my* reason, and all *my* senses, and still preserves them; in addition thereto, clothing and shoes, meat and drink, house and homestead, wife and children, fields, cattle, and all *my* goods; that He provides *me* richly and daily with all that *I* need to support this body and life, protects *me* from all danger, and guards *me* and preserves *me* from all evil; and all this out of pure, fatherly, divine goodness and mercy, without any merit or worthiness in me; for all which I owe it to Him to thank, praise, serve, and obey Him. This is most certainly true."

The Second Article. "I believe that Jesus Christ, true God,

begotten of the Father from eternity, and also true man, born of the Virgin Mary, is *my* Lord, who has redeemed *me,* a lost and condemned creature, purchased and won [delivered] *me* from all sins, from death, and from the power of the devil, not with gold and silver, but with His holy, precious blood and with His innocent suffering and death, in order that *I* may be [wholly] His own, and live under Him in His kingdom, and serve Him in everlasting righteousness, innocence, and blessedness, even as He is risen from the dead, lives and reigns to all eternity. This is most certainly true."

The Third Article. "I believe that *I* cannot by *my* own reason or strength believe in Jesus Christ *my* Lord, or come to Him; but the Holy Ghost has called *me* by the Gospel, enlightened *me* with his gifts, sanctified and kept *me* in the faith; even as He calls, gathers, enlightens, and sanctifies the whole Christian Church on earth, and keeps it with Jesus Christ in the one true faith; in which Christian Church He forgives daily and richly all sins to *me* and all believers, and at the last day will raise up *me* and all the dead, and will give to *me* and to all believers in Christ everlasting life. This is most certainly true."[1]

The exposition is given in the form of a profession. The most striking feature of its style is the preponderance of pronouns of the first person singular (*I, me*) and the corresponding possessive adjective (*my*). To be sure, the word "I" necessarily occurs in a formula which is meant to be an individual's profession, originally used in the baptism of adults. Thus, the pertinent place of this word is in the formal statement of profession: "I believe." Moreover, an acknowledgment of an obligation may be added in the form of a vow, and here the use of the word "I" or "my" is also to the point, to express the idea, "Since I believe that God has done this it is *my* duty to behave accordingly. Luther's exposition contains the "I" in both sorts of context: "I believe . . . " and "I owe it to Him . . . " In addition, however, the words "I", "me", and "my" occur frequently within the text of the exposition, too: 25 times in the American version, 11 times in the German original. By this means all the contents of the profession are primarily or exclusively referred to the ego of the believer. Where the exposition speaks about other creatures or believers, it declares that what applies to the person professing the faith holds good of others also. This is linguistically expressed by "and" or by "even as" ("me and all creatures," "even as he calls . . . ," "to me and to all believers," "me and all the dead"). Only the paraphrase of the *Amen*, "This is most certainly true," repeated after each of the Articles, seems to avoid pointing to the believer's self. But this sentence is a mere formal avowal of the preceding statements, and these forcibly refer their factual content to the believer's ego. Hence it is precisely this reference that is emphasized as "most certainly true."

The turn to the ego within the act of faith marks a striking contrast between Luther's exposition and the text of the Creed. In the traditional formula there is no word to indicate such a reference. The Creed speaks exclusively of God's relation to the world as a whole, of His work, and of the Church as the all-embracing body of the redeemed. The Triune God effects creation, redemption, and sanctification, and to His universal design and dispensation the believer assents and submits by professing, "I believe." It is therefore not a mere accident but an intrinsic necessity of a self-forgetting submission that no "I" should occur within the content of the profession.

Luther has reversed this order. To his mind, God's relation to the whole of creation, to the world and the Church, seems to be secondary. Primary is the relation to the believer's self. In fact, the whole exposition hinges on this relation. It is therefore consistent that in Luther's translation and exposition of the Creed, the word "Catholic" does not occur. He replaces it by the word "Christian." But this adjective is redundant since there is no Church except the Christian one. The intrinsic reason for the omission is the predominance of the ego which precludes an appreciation of the Church's catholicity.

For Luther, faith in the Creator means, first and above all, "that God has made *me*." What God's creation implies for the professing individual, he expounds with popular eloquence and elaborate prolixity. God's relation to the world, on the other hand, is mentioned in three words only ("and all creatures"), as a sort of appendange to what is said regarding the believer's self. As products of creation, Luther specifies only such things and persons as are in a close relation to the person reciting the profession. Body, soul, eyes, ears, all limbs, reason, all senses, clothing, shoes, meat and drink, house and homestead, wife and children, fields, cattle, all goods: all this has been created by God — for the believer's self. Moreover, God is active in supporting and preserving and protecting — the believer's self.

The Second Article correctly states the traditional doctrines of Christ's two natures, his preexistence and incarnation, the redemption he wrought by dying on the Cross, and his resurrection and exaltation. But the emphasis of the statements has been shifted. The Creed is centered on the truths about Jesus Christ alone. Luther's exposition construes the christological mysteries as attributes of the grammatical subject, Jesus Christ, of whom Luther then predicates that he "is my Lord." The possessive adjective "my" brings the christological facts into a relation to the believer's self. Luther then goes on to describe the redemption proper in long secondary clauses, dependent on "my Lord." He depicts the passion of Christ with forcible elaboration, and he represents it as having happened for the benefit of the believer's self. Other believers are not mentioned at all in this Article. The exposition then makes the reciter profess that he will attain final consummation. Christ's resurrection and exaltation belonged to the central contents of the profession in primitive Christianity. But Luther's exposition, by a striking "even as," appends these facts to the reciter's assertion of his salvation, thus explaining them primarily as a guarantee of the believer's eternal beatitude. All this inevitably leads the believer to focus his attention not on Christ alone but on the Redeemer's *relation to him*.

In the Third Article of the Creed one of the objects of faith specially proposed is the Church. Yet Luther's exposition makes the Church appear as a sort of appendage to the ego, by means of the conjunctions "and" and "even as" ("even as he calls . . . ," "to me and all believers," "me and all the dead") — much like the way he spoke of the creation and preservation of the world in expounding the First Article. Thus, even his interpretation of the Church starts from, and is centered upon, the ego. Consequently, those who have been instructed according to Luther's Catechism quite naturally come to believe that the Church is primarily and essentially an association of individuals gathered for the benefit of each individual. As the purpose of this gathering, Luther's exposition mentions the preservation of the faith and the remission of sin, which is given in the Church.

At the end of the Third Article, Luther repeats what he had already said in his comment on the Second Article. The reciter has once more to state with unrestricted assurance that he — and all those who have the same faith — will attain "everlasting life." This repetition sheds as much light on Luther's fundamental intention, as does the consistent reference of all the contents of the faith to the believer's self. Luther wishes to bring it home to the learner that "it is most certainly true" that he will be saved if he believes so.

A significant omission serves the same purpose. The Creed includes a statement about the Last Judgment. Now if a man profess that Christ will come "to judge the living and the dead," he has to reckon with the possibility of his being found guilty and thus he may lose his assurance as to attaining the ultimate goal. Consequently, Luther's exposition leaves the Last Judgment unexplained. What he meant by omitting this in the exposition, becomes still clearer when we compare the *Small Catechism* with other expositions of the Creed Luther composed. In 1520 he published the *Short Form,* which is his earliest catechism, and in 1529 his *Large Catechism,* destined for the use of pastors and teachers, as a companion to the *Small Catechism.* Both these catechisms treat of the Last Judgment. But in the *Short Form* it is "our foes and adversaries" who will be condemned, and the believer here states, without reservation, that Christ will come "to save *me* and all believers."[2] The *Large Catechism* says that Christ "will separate *us* from the wicked world . . . "[3] These statements show that the omission of the Last Judgment in the *Small Catechism* does not imply a tacit rejection of this article of faith. Rather, the believer is taught to be convinced that he will not be found guilty if and in so far as he believes that he will not be tried. Surely this conviction is easier to gain if reflection on the Last Judgment is not stirred up. Luther's pedagogical instinct chose this method in the *Small Catechism* since in this booklet he meant to instruct children and common people. The Creed, which every Christian learns by heart, does mention the Last

Judgment. Yet Luther effectively neutralized this teaching in his exposition by replacing it with emphatic and unqualified and repeated statements of assurance.

Luther's attitude toward the dogma of the Last Judgment was quite complicated. This article marks the point where dogmatic faith tended to clash with existential faith in Luther's spiritual life. His thought was to a large extent a continual and strained effort to evade the deadly stress.

Occasionaly, Luther could expound the faith even without making the believer explicitly assert that he will attain beatitude. In an appendix to his bulky controversial treatise of 1528, "On the Lord's Supper," he gives an elaborate profession of faith in which he says, while speaking of the End of All Things, that after the Resurrection "everyone will receive his due in his body according to his merit, and thus the pious will live with Christ to all eternity and the wicked will die to all eternity with the devil and his angels."[4] Yet this does not imply a doctrine different from that of the Catechisms. First, the "pious ones," according to Luther, are doubtless those whose faith is in accordance with the teaching of the Catechisms. Second, the treatise in question polemizes against sects that had assimilated Luther's doctrine of faith but differed from him in the way they had developed the doctrine. It is quite natural that the controversialist did not feel inclined in such a situation to emphasize what he had in common with his opponents. He, himself, explicitly states that he is annexing a profession of faith to the treatise because he has seen "that sectarianism and heresy are increasing ever more." Thus it is clear that his opponents are here not Catholics but Protestant sectarians, and this entailed a different way of exposition. The profession annexed to the treatise, "On the Lord's Supper," is not the only text in Luther's works that formulates ideas in deliberate opposition to certain adversaries.

2. Reflexivity

Luther's exposition of the Creed teaches the believer to profess the faith and at the same time to look back at his own self. This is not just a pastoral suggestion compensated elsewhere by other doctrinal statements. Rather, Luther intends to present here an exercise in the sort of faith which he conceived to be *justifying*. The reference to the ego is not a meditation beside the act of faith but a part, and the essential part, of the act itself. Within the very act of faith, the ego bends back on itself. This sort of faith may fittingly be called *reflexive*.

Pure Christian faith is an act of obedient self-donation. The believer surrenders himself to the transcendent God in the assent of adoration. This makes him understand creation and the Church as parts of God's saving dispensation and assigns to him his place and his shelter in the order of Providence. Thus he can trust in God the Creator, the Redeemer and the Sanctifier, and move spiritually away from himself in love for God. The more his faith becomes mature through loving cooperation with God's grace, the less is it possible for him to turn his attention back to himself within the act of faith.

Reflexive faith, on the other hand, is comparable to a missile launched toward a target with contrivances devised to make it rebound and return to its starting point which is thus its ultimate aim. The act of reflexive faith is directed to the Divine Person of Christ, but it is intended to recoil on the believer's ego in order to evoke in him a consciousness of his own relation with God, a consciousness of consolation and salvation. This intensive act of consciousness singles out the ego from the general dispensation of God. While non-reflexive faith primarily contemplates the more comprehensive dispensation, reflexive faith strives to secure God's gift to the individual believer.

Luther also taught his new conception of faith outside the practical and pastoral context of his catechisms. He often expounded it in theological arguments with all desirable explicitness. A few quotations from some of his works, written in 1519 and 1535, may provisionally suffice as examples. In his 1519 *Commentary on Galatians* he wrote: "It is of no avail for you to believe that Christ has been given for the sins of other saints but to doubt this with regard to your sins. For this [general truth] the impious and the devils also believe.[5] Rather you should assume with constant trust that he has been given up for your sins, too, and *that you are one of those* for whose sins he has been given. This is the faith that justifies you (*haec fides te justificat*) and

will make Christ dwell, live, and rule in you."[6] "Believe that
he will be salvation and mercy *to you,* and it will be so without
any doubt."[7] In a sermon preached on June 29, 1519, Luther said:
"If a man doubts and is not firmly convinced that he has a merciful God, he does not have him. *As he believes, so he has.* Therefore nobody can possibly know that he is in God's grace and that
God is propitious to him except through faith. *If he believes it,
he is blessed; if not, he is condemned.* For such assurance and
good conscience is the right . . . faith that God's grace works in
us."[8] In a disputation "On Faith' 'held in 1535, Luther proposed
the theses: "It is that '*For me*' or '*For us*' which, if believed,
constitutes this *true* faith and distinguishes it from any other sort
of faith which only accepts that certain events did happen."[9] "This
is the faith which alone justifies us."[10]

From the last months of 1517 to the end of his life, Luther never
tired of repeating the idea expressed in the above quotations. According to him, what properly justifies is not simply faith in God
or Christ. Only the reflection, qualified by certitude, that God's
salvific deed is meant *"for me"* works salvation, and this reflection
brings about its effect infallibly. The quotations describe this
sort of faith as "assurance" or "trust." We will have to examine
whether it really is trust.

Luther himself denoted the faith taught by him as "apprehensive faith" in the sense of "seizing faith" (*fides apprehensiva*).[11]
This means that faith grasps not only the message of salvation
but salvation itself or even Christ himself. We will have to
consider this important term more in detail when discussing
Luther's doctrine of charity. For the time being, it may be useful
to mark off Luther's conception from a different application of
the same term. In the Song of Songs (3, 4), the Bride says: "I
held him, and would not let him go." This passage has inspired
a conception of "seizing faith" in mysticism. St. Gregory of
Nyssa in his exposition of the passage writes: "By faith I found
the Beloved One and I shall not let him go again, keeping fast to
him whom I found with the seizure of faith, until he has come
into my chamber."[12] The similarity, and at the same time the
dissimilarity, of this idea to that of Luther's is most significant.
The similarity is indicative of Luther's proximity to mysticism,

which we will have to take into account when investigating the genesis of his new conception of faith and when treating of his later spirituality. The dissimilarity is constituted by the novelty of Luther's conception. In Gregory's thought (as in all sound Catholic spirituality from 1 Cor 13 onward) the grasp of faith is included in the comprehensive movement of love, in which the soul is seeking Christ the Bridegroom. She had already thought that she had reached the end of her hopes and attained union with the aim of her longings. Yet she then experiences that this participation in the Beloved is a night, a darkness, in which the object of her love eludes any grasp by mental efforts. So she finds herself as far from perfection as a person who has not even started, and in this night love holds the Beloved One by faith alone. Luther's doctrine, however, rejects the biblical subordination of faith to love and rules out the inclusion of faith in the movement of love, as we shall see in Chapter IV. His term "apprehensive faith" would therefore be misunderstood if equated with similar terms used by mystics.

A pregnant expression of the reflexivity of Luther's faith is its description as *faith in one's own faith*. This description is suggested by Luther's exhortation "to have faith in the believed Christ." He means to say that a man who does already believe in Christ must believe a second time to apply the content of faith (*factum*) to himself, thus "making use" of the believed "fact" (*usus facti*).[13] The "utilization" of the believed fact is another term to signify the same act that Luther elsewhere denotes as "apprehensive faith."

Only in this sense will we use the term "reflexive faith" in the present book. Reflection on the bearing of faith upon the believer's self is not, as such, reflexive faith. Reflection may accompany, precede, or follow the act of faith without identifying itself with faith proper or conceiving itself to be the justifying element in faith. Devout Christians have at all times meditated on the relevance of faith for their destiny, and this has prompted them to acts of repentance, thanksgiving, love, hope, joy, and to make good resolutions.

In antiquity, examples of self-reflection abound in the works of St. Augustine, especially in those of his earlier period and in the

Confessions. Less known, perhaps, is the fact that St. Ambrose also practiced self-reflection. In meditating on the story of the birth of Jesus Christ, the saint writes: "Thus that poverty is my patrimony, and the weakness of the Lord is my strength . . . It is I whom that weeping of the whimpering infant purifies and his tears have washed away my crimes."[14] Such reflections not only "seem to anticipate by centuries what was called *devotio moderna* in a certain epoch of the Middle Ages,"[15] but they also recall some of Luther's meditations on the Incarnation. St. Ambrose is realizing that his own self is concerned by the events of Christ's birth and life and suffering; yet his reflection is completely different from reflexive faith. The difference becomes clear when we compare the saint's words with Christmas sermons preached by Luther. In 1522 he claims: "This is the right faith, full of grace, which God's word and work *demands*: that you should believe firmly that Christ is given to *you* and his birth . . . occurred for *your* benefit."[16] In 1530: "The faith *must* be added that the Savior is born *for you.*"[17] Luther *insists* on the believer's realizing that the Incarnation has happened *for him,* and he warns that the faith would fail to justify the believer *unless* it include the explicit apprehension, "It has happened *for me.*" It is these two features that distinguish reflexive faith from religious self-reflection.

In the Middle Ages, outstanding examples of self-reflection can be found in the works of St. Bernard and his school and, of course, in the *devotio moderna* of Thomas a Kempis. We will have to examine a relevant passage from St. Bernard when inquiring into the origin of Luther's new conception (Chapter II, Section 1).

In his pre-Protestant period Luther himself presented some instances in point. In his Gloss on Psalm 6, written in 1513, he says: "Imagine your Lord, your Redeemer, kneeling before the Father in meekest charity and piety, laden with your sins and those of the whole world, weeping bitterly for them and indignantly detesting them. It is you for whom such a great Mediator is praying so fervently. What, therefore, will be your response? Will you not pray and weep with him, who is praying and weeping for you and for your misery?"[18] On St. Lawrence's feast, in 1516, he preached: "If we believe that he has created us, that he protects and educates us and makes everything created serve us — if, I say, we believe that this is really true, how can it happen that we should not love him with all our heart?"[19] On January 1, 1517, he preached: "There is the Lord, lying in the manger, freezing for me, who then suffered troubles throughout his life, and finally prayed for those with whom he had every reason to be angry — and I, dust that I am, should I not stop being angry with my brother and should I not rather pray for him and return good for evil?"[20] These meditations are of special value to illustrate the difference from Luther's later thought. Here too the *"for me"* is emphasized, but there is no trace of the idea, characteristic of reflexive faith, that the believer *lays a claim* to the redemption and tries to *appropriate* it to himself by apprehending it as being *for me*. Instead, the reflection on the self serves as an incentive to intensify piety and penitence and humility and love for Christ and brotherly love. To be sure, even Luther's exposition of the Creed in the *Small Catechism* can be construed — and has certainly been interpreted by many readers, especially Catholics — as a meditation in which the self-reflection merely serves to prompt gratitude and joy. But such an interpretation, though bringing out a feature that is doubtless also implied, fails to grasp the author's main intention. The Catechism presents a practical exercise, not theory, even though it presupposes a theory.

Self-reflection, though not absent in previous epochs, has in the last centuries attained an intensity and diffusion that make it appear a distinctive feature of the mind of modern man. It is a potentiality of human nature and like all sound human gifts, it can be utilized for the glory of God. It can be applied with profit in genuinely Catholic spirituality, life, and theology. The lectures and sermons of Luther's pre-Protestant period were a promise. He failed to fulfill it. So it was for others to carry through the experiment. St. Ignatius Loyola evolved his *Spiritual Exercises*. St. Francis of Sales (1557-1622) taught a "layman's spirituality," worthier of this designation than certain projects of our days, because it was based on love for God and thus eminently spiritual. The reformers of the Carmelite Order in Spain,

St. Teresa of Avila (1515-1582) and St. John of the Cross (1542-1591), developed the doctrine of mysticism to classical perfection. The saintly teachers of the French Oratory — Bérulle (1575-1629), Condren (1588-1641), and Olier (1608-1657) — elaborated a method of adorational meditation in which man was to establish communion with Christ. In all these and other types of spirituality that arose after the divisive Reformation self-reflection was included but duly subordinated to love, obedience, and adoration. There is thus ample evidence that Catholicism can make good use of the modern trend to self-reflection.

Luther's reflexive faith, however, was an aberration.[21] Instead of making the modern trend of thought subservient to the spiritual life, he, conversely, presented a special variety of this trend as the only genuine and legitimate form of religion. The crucial point is therefore not the existence or legitimacy of the modern tendency to self-reflection but the way this tendency is applied in practice in religious life and theology. Luther did unreflectingly what many theologians today do deliberately: like him, they make the spirit of the epoch the criterion of what should be held and practiced in the Church and what not.

At Luther's time the new mentality was not yet widespread. But the doctrine of reflexive faith certainly contributed to the diffusion of the modern way of thinking. For this doctrine gave the modern mind an absolute importance inasmuch as it made the success or failure of a self-reflection decisive for man's attaining or losing his ultimate goal. Thus Lutheranism and the modern way of thinking mutually promoted one another. This explains much of the success of Lutheranism — and of Protestantism in general, since all varieties of Protestantism assimilated the new doctrine of faith.

Luther's conviction that an anthropocentric turn was the essential aspect of faith sometimes produced coarse statements. In 1520 he wrote, "Here it should be borne in mind that there are two sorts of belief. First, (belief) *about* God, which means that I believe that it is true what is said of God. This is similar to believing that it is true what is said of the Turks, of the Devil (or of hell). This belief is knowledge or consideration rather than faith. Second, there is belief *in* God. This means: I not only believe that it is true what is said of God, but I put my trust in him, I decide and resolve to act with him (i.e., I enter into a relationship with him), and I believe without any doubt that he will be and do to *me* that which is said of him."[22]

These words at first sight seem to describe genuine and living trust. A person who resolves to enter into a relationship with God certainly has trust and faith in him. But this is not all. Two points in Luther's text are significant. First, faith naturally includes "knowledge" and "consideration" or contemplation. Now for Luther these are no more than a basis, indispensable indeed, but in themselves of no greater value than information about any uninteresting or even contemptible subject. Yet it is these features — knowledge and, especially, contemplation — that constitute the orientation of faith *to God*, which is essential to real faith. Luther's depreciation of them pave the way for a development which eventually was to dispense with dogma altogether. Second, what matters according to Luther, is the belief that God "will be and do *to me* that which is said of him." This shows graphically that the direction of faith to God is merely a presupposition for the turn to the own self. The facts that are "said of God" form, as it were, a reflecting surface capable of throwing back the ray of faith to its starting-point, the believer's ego. Only when the ray has returned to its starting-point is the act of faith a success. The disparagement of the contemplative orientation toward God is in perfect correspondence with the emphasis on the return to the ego in the act of faith.

Luther's discrimination between the two sorts of faith recalls the traditional distinction between *credere Deum* (to believe that God exists), *credere Deo* (to give credence to God), and *credere in Deum* (to have faith in God). A comparison of the traditional doctrine with Luther's explanation is most illustrative of the novelty of his conception. The difference of the three modes of belief is explained by St. Thomas Aquinas[23] in a systematic and psychological way, whereas St. Augustine's interpretation is more spiritual.[24] Luther probably did not know much of the *Summa* of Aquinas, but, being an Augustinian monk, he was well acquainted with the works of the greatest Father of the Latin Church. This fact, as well as the greater originality and depth of Augustine's thought, recommends a comparison with St. Augustine. Augustine agrees with Luther in attributing only little value to the mere belief that Christ exists. He says: "The devils also believed that Christ existed," and there are many reminiscences of this allusion to James 2, 19, in Luther's works.[25] The difference between the saint and the Reformer lies in their interpretation of the preposition *"in"* occurring in the phrase "to believe *in* God." According to St. Augustine, this *"in"* indicates the plenitude of faith, which is realized in its interpenetration with hope and love. Every close reader of the New Testament and of the Apostolic Fathers will recognize that the saint is here in perfect accordance with an ancient and essential tradition of Christian spirituality. Augustine preaches: "He believes (has faith) in Christ who hopes in Christ and also loves Christ . . . Therefore Christ enters into him who has faith in Christ, through his believing in Christ, and he becomes in a certain manner united to Him and is made a member of His Body. This cannot happen unless hope and also charity are added." At another place, he distinguishes the construction with the dative case (*credere ei,* give credence to Him) from the construction with *in.* Here he says that it is not enough to give credence to God, "for the devils also believed him." We believe (give credence to) a human being, but regarding God we should have faith *in* him. This is the faith that justifies the sinner. "What is it, then, 'to believe in him?' It is to love through faith, to have charity by faith, to enter into him by faith, and to be incorporated among his members." Thus faith, essentially permeated with hope and charity, is not a mere individual act but has an ecclesial dimension. It connotes union with Christ in the Church: Christ in us, we in Him. Augustine's interpretation is in accord with the grammatical meaning of the preposition *in,* which, construed with the accusative, expresses a *movement toward* (God or Christ) and involves a *going out* (from the ego). If we consider all this, Luther's explanation appears strikingly strained. He interprets the *in* as implying exactly the opposite of its grammatical meaning. For he takes it as an encouragement for the believer, not to start out from but to turn back to, his own self: "God will be and do *to me* that which is said of him." The interpetration of faith with hope and love as well as the ecclesial dimension are lost sight of. Thus in spite of the similarity of the statements, Luther's depreciation of mere "knowledge and consideration" also indicates an attitude different from Augustine's warning against a mere belief that Christ or God exists. After all, the saint's exposition of Scripture are full of "consideration" of the mysteries of faith. These meditations are the theologian's practice of "loving faith" (*credendo amare*). They turn to the individual believer only to remind him of what he owes to God and never envisage him outside of his inclusion in the Mystical Body of Christ.

It seems that Luther himself did not notice his drift toward anthropocentric religion. He was sincerely convinced that his faith was looking at Christ alone. The 1531-35 *Commentary on Galatians* says: "You should place Christ before your eyes in such a way that you do not perceive anything besides him."[26] But Luther was here under a delusion. Whenever he described the content of faith, he did not fail to mention the believer's self as included in that content. His attention was directed to Christ only in so far as the believer is related to the Redeemer. Thus the same passage of this commentary states: "I believe in Jesus Christ, the Son of God, who suffered, was crucified, and died *for me* and in whose wounds I see *my* sin." This reference to the believer's self is all the more remarkable as it is part of a comment on Gal. 3, 28, "You are *all one* [i.e. one living being, *heis*; not one thing, *hen*] in Christ Jesus." Luther explains the word "all" as signifying that distinctions between persons are meaningless to God; then he goes on to speak of the *individual's* union with Christ. St. Paul's text conveys the idea of a union of all in the one living reality which is the Body of Christ, the Church. But Luther interprets it as implying that each individual, without discrimination of person, is one with Christ.

Thus Luther's faith is not "faith in an objective salvation or in him who gives it but faith immediately in the own salvation of the believer."[27] Accordingly Luther can occasionally describe faith even with exclusive reference to the believer's self, without any mention of God or Christ, in saying, for instance, that faith is "a firm grasp and a constant awareness of justice and salvation."[28] From here, there is a very short distance to Bultmann's definition of faith as "existential self-understanding"[29] or to Ebeling's remark that "faith is essentially this certitude concerning the future (of existence)."[30] The anthropocentrism of modern existentialist theology, which can speak of faith in terms merely of human existence, is preformed in Luther's conception and some of his statements already bring it out explicitly.

From a note that one of his pupils took down it appears that Luther himself, at the age of sixty, used the word "reflexive faith," *fides reflexa,* in a remark at table. The note runs: "Our nature is such that we would fain have *fidem reflexam.* We would like to grip it and put it in our bosom, but that does not happen *in vita corporali.*"[31] As the context shows, Luther is referring here primarily to a desire to gain assurance through intellectual understanding. Anyway, it is a sort of faith which is supposed to bring about assurance. Now was Luther's "apprehensive faith" very different from that "grip" which he criticized in the table remark? Does it make a great difference whether the "grip" is sought as an intellectual grasping or as a feeling of certitude? May we, therefore, assume that toward the end of his life Luther himself sometimes felt that his conception of faith was objectionable? True enough, the opinion he criticizes is not exactly the same which he had been teaching. But his criticism may be an indication both of his doubt and of an attempt to stifle it — by representing the "grip" as something different from the kind of faith he had been inculcating.

Luther has often been labeled an individualist or subjectivist and no less often has this characterization been denied. His teachings seem to lend support both to the assertion and to the denial. This paradoxical fact shows that neither of the two terms accurately describes his attitude. Indeed, there are kinds of religious subjectivism and individualism in which a believer does not bend back on his own self within the act of faith. On the other hand, reflexivity of faith can very well coexist with practical altruism and spirit of fellowship as well as with a certain dogmatic objectivism. And precisely this, is Luther's case. He was not the sort of individualist who did not care for social communication. Time and again, his teaching enjoin social obligations. Furthermore, Luther was not a subjectivist in the sense that he left it to the discretion of each individual to accept or reject any traditional dogma. He differed from the "enthusiasts" in attributing to Scripture and the sacraments a more objective meaning than they did — though he agreed with them in the doctrine of reflexivity, which they had learned from him. But he cannot simply be described as an objectivist either. The problem is complex. We will have to return to it in other contexts.

3. Assertiveness

The believer who follows Luther's teaching seeks a certitude that refers to his whole person. He strives to be certain that his sins are forgiven and his other works are agreeable to God. As early as 1518 Luther warns that he who doubts of his works being agreeable to God "is committing a sin."[32] A year or two later he defines faith as "a lively and undoubted belief that makes a man absolutely certain of his being pleasing to God." Faith is the conviction that God is "propitious in the matter of good deeds and forgiving toward what is wrong."[33] There are statements in which Luther expressly says that it is man's confidence that *constitutes* the acceptability or agreeableness of his person to God, and he expresses this idea both in positive and negative terms. Positively, he teaches: "If you find your heart confident that the work is agreeable to God then it *is* good."[34] Negatively: If "the conscience does not dare to know for certain or be confident that this or that is agreeable to God then it is *certain* that it does *not* please him."[35] "If you think God is wrathful then he *is* so."[36] In brief summary: "As (your heart) feels so Christ is behaving."[37] "*As a man believes so he has.*"[38]

There are many passages in Luther's works which do not explicitly refer to faith's bending back on its subject but which represent God's attitude toward man as dependent on what man thinks that attitude is like. The reflexive movement of the act of faith takes the form of *assertion*. In his 1531-35 *Commentary on Galatians* Luther urged time and again that the believer should "assert with certitude" (*certo statuere*) that his person is agreeable to God. The man-related or even man-centered trend of the new doctrine becomes most conspicuous in this exhortation. Yet Luther himself did not perceive the anthropocentric implication. He emphasized that the assertion was not based on what man did but on what Christ had done for him, so he was convinced that it was precisely his way of believing in God's word that "gave God the greatest honor."[39] But upon the belief that redemption is a pure gift, Luther superimposes the assertion of his claim for it. In his last lectures, he taught: "Faith snatches (*arripit*) the merit of Christ and asserts (or posits, *statuit*) that we have been liberated by his death."[40] Now a man who wants to "snatch" or claim or arrogate a gift is no longer recognizing it as a pure gift. The part of man in salvation is here overstrained and overemphasized. Luther did not notice this.

However, the new concept of faith inescapably initiated a development in which religion became at first man-oriented and eventually man-centered. The reflexivity, apprehensivity, and assertiveness of this sort of faith constituted the seed of anthropocentrism in religion and of idealism in philosophy. The seed has grown exuberantly. In theology, its most stately growth was the system of Schleiermacher. In philosophy, after sprouting in tenets of Descartes, Kant, and others, it put forth glamorous flowers in the thought of Fichte and Hegel, whose systems in turn, through the intermediary of Joseph Maréchal, engendered anthropological theology in modern Catholicism. The most radical form of anthropocentrism, asymptotically approximating to atheism, has been reached in Protestant existentialism — whose advocates emphatically profess their allegiance and indebtedness to Martin Luther. They use the term "justifying faith" as if it meant faith in one's own justification. They can talk about justification without even mentioning God and they can define faith in terms merely of human existence. Ebeling, for instance, says that "faith is existence's being determined as existence in this world."[41] To understand this, it has to be borne in mind that "existence" in the language of existentialists means *individual human* existence, or the self conceived as a chain of events.

The man-oriented turn appears not only in Luther's descriptions of the nature of faith but even in statements he made on God. For instance, in the exposition of the First Commandment in his *Large Catechism* he defines God thus: "A God is called that from which [not: he from whom!] a man is to hope to obtain all good and to which he is to take refuge in all needs. Thus, to *have* a God is nothing but to *trust* and *believe* in him wholeheartedly . . . The trust and belief of the heart makes both God and idol."[42] Now Luther surely had a most vivid realization of the transcendent reality of God. Nevertheless, his notion of faith as being essentially reflexive, apprehensive and assertive made it possible for him to define God in terms of human existence. .

Luther's 1531-35 *Commentary on Galatians* attempts to prove the necessity of assertion by theological arguments. Luther reasons thus: Christ pleases God, and we cling to Christ; consequently we must also be agreeable to God. Moreover, God has sent the Spirit of his Son into our hearts. Now Christ is certain that he pleases God. Consequently we, too, who are in possession of his Spirit, must be certain that we are agreeable to God.[43]

The premises of this argumentation are surely in agreement with Holy Scripture. But Luther does not have regard to all that is relevant in this connection. He leaves out of account man's personal relationship to Christ, which includes reverence, love, and active obedience toward his commandments. If all this is duly considered, it is no longer possible to conclude that man can and must assert his being agreeable to God. We cannot prejudge that all our behavior toward God was and is and will be acceptable to him. There is the grave possibility that we may "receive the grace of God in vain" (2 Cor. 6, 1). By no means can it be demonstrated from Scripture that our being agreeable to God depends on our asserting that we are so.

The doctrine of reflexive faith not only demands that one perform the act of assertion but also that one retain the prerequisite of the act, which is the content of faith. This content is not accepted because the Church teaches it and not necessarily in the form in which the Church proposes it. Rather, the apprehending assertion involves an individual view of the content of faith, namely a view that makes it appear *plausible*. Only such a view seems to ensure certitude as the success of the assertion. Luther's exposition of the Creed is an attempt to train Christians to impress the outlines of an individual view referring all the contents of faith to the believer's self.

What this exposition presented in 1529 in the form of an exercise is the condensation of a teaching elaborated through more than ten years. After his separation from the Catholic Church, Luther inculcated time and again that the believer himself must judge, or decide upon, the content of faith: "that a man be certain, each one for himself, accounting for our faith . . . For you will not be condemned or saved through another's doctrine, be it true or false, but only through your faith. Therefore let everyone teach whatever he likes; you have to see to what you believe, at your own ultimate peril or for your own ultimate profit."[44] Thus Luther wrote in 1523. Two years later he speaks of an "interior judgment" (*judicium interius*) which enables "each man to judge, and to decide upon, the doctrines and opinions of all, (since he is) enlightened by the Holy Spirit or the special gift of God with regard to himself and his own individual salvation. . . . This pertains to faith and is necessary for every Christian, even for a layman."[45]

Certitude of salvation, to use the terminology of Christian mystics, is a kind of *consolation*. But consolation is not available at will. The grip of assertion is certainly the most unsuitable means to secure it. It is therefore no wonder that Luther is continually fluctuating between the insistence on certitude and the avowal of incertitude. In 1520 he taught that certitude was easy to attain. Faith, he wrote, is "the highest of all works." It deletes "daily sins," and even if a "deadly fall" should happen, "nevertheless faith rises again and does not doubt that the sin is already gone."[46] In later writings, however, Luther forcibly described how the Divine Law frightens man's conscience and how consoling faith arises from this terror but has constantly to struggle against the trial or "temptation" of incertitude and thus to strive for certitude, ever anew. He even warns against losing the consciousness of sin too early. For otherwise a man will fall into "security," which is detestable. Thus the *Scholia on Isaiah* (1532) say: "Christians are people who have an overwhelming awareness of death and of the power of sin. But . . . in the very awareness of sin and death they nevertheless somehow cling to Christ, they do not renounce his word, but suffer and remain in Christ."[47] They have perpetually to *train themselves* in feeling: "You have no sins though you have sinned, but your sins cling to Christ."[48]

It is "a tremendous *labor* for faith" to "overcome the con-science."[49] The Galatians' commentary admonishes: "Everyone should *accustom himself* to assert with certitude that he is in a state of grace . . . If, however, he feel that he is doubting, he should practice faith and struggle against doubt and strive for certitude."[50]

The last four quotations are taken from editions of lectures made by Luther's pupils. Besides these editions, notes are extant which the pupils took while the Doctor was lecturing. The basic ideas are the same in the notes and the editions. But it is inter-esting to note that the editions emphasize still more than the notes do the necessity of "asserting with certitude" in order to put down the oppressing reality of incertitude. This seems to indicate that a method which could not but fail was at least as unsuccessful with the pupils as it was with the Doctor.

Assertion of one's salvation is also the solution that Luther proposes for the problem of perseverance to the end. In the col-lection of sermons which he published in 1522, he says that a man "must not doubt or waver in the belief that he is one of those to whom grace and mercy is given, and . . . he must freely assert that he is . . . certain to win beatitude . . . (But) there is fear and anxiety as to his remaining thus till the end . . . (His) faith boasts not of works nor of itself but only of God and his grace. And this grace cannot and will not leave him as long as that boasting lasts. But how long it will last, he does not know. If . . . the boasting ceases then grace also ceases."[51]

The word "boasting" is here used to render the German *pochen*. This word means "proudly to lay a claim to something." It is an emphatic variant of what Luther's Latin expresses by *certo statuere*.

The special import of the passage quoted consists in its stress-ing that grace is present *as often* and *as long* as the assertion of its presence is maintained. Consequently, unceasing assertion of one's being in God's grace is perseverance till the end.

On the one hand, Luther enjoins man's mental effort of assertion as the means to attain the salvific certitude, on the other hand, he insists with the same emphasis that man "cannot by his own reason or strength believe in Jesus Christ" (as the

Small Catechism says) but that faith is "a divine work in us,"[52] "a gift of the Holy Spirit."[53] Did he notice the contradiction between the two doctrines, and did he make any attempt to reconcile them? The answer is surprising: he does not seem to have noticed the contrariety. True, if we may believe the editor of his 1531-35 *Commentary on Galatians* — and we are justified in regarding the edition as a reliable rendering of Luther's views — Luther's sensitive conscience did tell him what the assertion of one's own salvation amounted to, namely, to presumption.[54] But he thought that for the sake of his salvation he was obliged to stifle even this remorse. So we can only say that Luther's doctrine included the idea that faith is a gift of God precisely in its reflexivity and assertiveness. When he said that it was the Holy Spirit who infuses faith into him who is hearing the gospel,[55] he was certainly understanding this faith as reflexive.

Especially instructive in this connection is the interpretation that Luther gives of the First Commandment of the decalogue in his *Treatise on Good Works,* published in 1520. He contends that this commandment enjoins faith. His description of the nature of faith includes remarkable remnants of his early theology of the cross (which we will have to sketch in a later chapter). But the predominant feature of faith is the confidence that all one's works either are agreeable to, or condoned by, God. Thus it is the reflex assertion, "I am acceptable to God," that constitutes the genuineness of faith. And this kind of faith, Luther claims, "comes from Christ alone" and, like the Holy Spirit, is given on hearing the gospel.[56]

In another text, Luther cautions against a faith that man "makes for himself out of his own power."[57] This warning makes one wonder all the more that Luther did not perceive the problem involved in the assertion of one's own state of grace. Is such reflex assertion really included in the faith that is a gift of God, or is it not rather a type of faith that man "makes for himself"? This query calls for a recourse to the source of all Christian theology, namely to the New Testament. The question then will be: Does the New Testament teach, or justify, or admit of, reflexive and assertive faith? We will examine this problem especially in the third chapter. Two aspects, however, may be discussed here.

Luther's exhortations intend to develop precisely the reflexivity of faith. On the other hand, the assertive reference to one's own self constitutes the justifying element in faith. Luther thus heedlessly presupposes that it is a mental effort that makes faith justifying. We may interpret this as an unconscious adaptation of the Church's doctrine that man has to cooperate with God's grace for his salvation. When Luther passionately rejected this doctrine, he was unreflectingly shifting its content to the realm of psychology. The New Testament and the Church teach that salvation, which is a gift of God, is actualized by man in virtue of the grace he has received. Similarly, Luther describes justifying faith as a divine gift and at the same time as the success of a mental effort.

Both Catholics and Protestants are agreed that faith is a gift of God. Now is it possible that a man may misuse such a gift? If we follow the teaching of the New Testament, we must reply that it is surely possible. St. Paul thanks God for the grace of God which is given to the Corinthians (1 Cor. 1, 4); yet, in the same Epistle, he censures the Corinthians severely for serious misuse of the charisms which he admits they really possess. A man who adopts a heresy — and the Corinthians were on the point of falling into heresies — has certainly received his faith as a gift from God, but his deliberate option for the heresy is a misuse of the gift. Man has the liberty, which involves a grave responsibility, of making right or wrong use of a gift of God, even of a spiritual gift. If a scrutiny of the New Testament should reveal that reflexivity and assertiveness are alien to the nature of faith, then these innovations of Luther's must involve a misuse of a gift of God. And it seems all the more necessary to investigate these features of Luther's doctrine since they have so seldom been considered, specially, and nonetheless have exerted an extraordinary power in the history of human thought.

4.   Reflexivity and a Personal Relation to Christ

Not only Protestants, but even Catholics, commonly take it for granted that Luther's notion of faith and of religion as a whole was eminently personalistic. Recent expositors of Luther's theology like Paul Althaus (1962),[58] Gerhard Ebeling (1964),[59] and

Friedrich Gogarten (1967)[60] have restated this view. But what Althaus understands by personalism is essentially the individualistic tendency prominent in some of Luther's statements. Gogarten finds the personalism of Luther's faith precisely in its reflexivity, and Ebeling's view virtually coincides with his. If these scholars are right, then personalism would amount to egocentricism and subjectivism. Ebeling, strangely enough, rules out love as the essential attitude of the human person to Christ.

For nearly half a century, philosophers and theologians have been reflecting much about the nature of the human self, or person. There is no unanimity among them, nor are the results of their reflections distinguished by logical clearness or systematic consistency. But even those who do not accept a modern notion of person will admit that it is proper to man to stand in relationships with other men which are not only ontological but also dynamic or ethical. These relationships we will call *interpersonal.* There are types of relationship that are more intrinsically linked to the nature of man or the selfhood of the self, and others that are less so.

Luther has often described faith as trust in God. Now trust is an interpersonal relationship of a high order. It presupposes freedom, which is constitutive of the spiritual nature of man. As a free, outgoing movement from one's own self, trust involves respect, or even reverence, for the freedom of the person in whom trust is placed. The trusting person is sure of what kind of action and behavior he can expect of the person whom he trusts, and what kind not. The ground of such certitude is solely his sympathetic and understanding nearness to the other person. If, however, he would seek to secure a profit from the other by means of his trusting him, then the relationship would become deranged. It would no longer be a relationship of one free self to another but an attempt to exploit the other. It would degenerate into egocentricism or selfishness. It is true that a person in whom I place my trust would not behave toward me in this or that way if he did not trust me and if he were not sure that I was trusting him. Nevertheless I would be perverting the relationship of trust if, through my very trust, I sought to make sure of a behavior of the person whom I am trusting. I would be disregarding the other's freedom and misusing his trust, for a self-profit or a self-assertion.

Now this is exactly what happens in reflexive faith. For here the believer seeks to secure Christ's attitude toward himself precisely by trusting Christ. His confidence, rather than being pure trust, includes the assertion of a claim which misinterprets itself as trust. Aspects of this derangement caused by Luther's conception of faith will be considered in later chapters, especially in connection with his doctrine of love and his doctrine of the sacraments. At the present stage of our investigation it may suffice to point out a few facts to illustrate the change in the relationship to Christ produced by reflexive faith.

One of the central teachings of the New Testament is the imitation of Christ, culminating in the exhortation to take up and carry one's cross (Mt. 16, 24; Lk. 14, 27, etc.). This implies, as St. Paul expounds, that one "share in his sufferings, becoming like him in his death, that if possible I may attain the resurrection from the dead" (Phil. 3, 10 f). It is a communion, much more intimate than any human relationship. For Christ, being God in his person, bestows on those who believe in him and love him a similarity with his human nature, in order to eventually elevate them to the state of his transfigured body in the glory of consummation (Phil. 3, 21; cf. 2 Cor. 4, 11; Rom. 8, 11).

St. Augustine has interpreted this redemptive communion by describing Christ as *sacramentum* and *exemplum*.[61] The two terms require some explanation. *Exemplum* signifies a manifest likeness, a type which is of the same kind as the antitype. Thus Christ's suffering and death are the *exemplum*, or likeness, of our own suffering, provided this is informed with the same spirit as was Christ's. This can be suffering for our brethren (see Col. 1, 24). It is an extension of Christ's witnessing for and response to the Father's love (martyrdom). Again, Christ's glorified body, risen from the dead, is the likeness or model, the pledge, and the efficacious sign of our future resurrection. In this sense his death and resurrection are *exemplum*. They are types, efficacious in the antitype.

Sacramentum, on the other hand, entails a hidden and therefore mysterious likeness. In regard to our interior life, Christ's suffering is not *exemplum* but *sacramentum* because here there is no direct or manifest likeness, the type not being of the same kind as the antitype. The *sacramentum* of Christ's suffering and death is appropriated through penance; the *sacramentum* of his resurrection through faith and the moral life. Here again, as in the case of *exemplum*, the type is *effective* in the antitype.

This schema of St. Augustine, surely an authentic interpretation of the New Testament, depicts an important feature of the interpersonal relationship between Christ and the believer. The Divine Person of Christ, in assuming a human nature and thus stooping down to mankind, offers a salvific likeness so that man through its mediation can reëstablish his relationship with God. Man responds to this initiative by faith and works, assimilating himself to the likeness more and more, until perfect resemblance with it (1 Jn. 3, 2) is granted him in the resurrection.

Luther, in his pre-Protestant period, often used St. Augustine's schema of *exemplum* and *sacramentum* in his notes, lectures, and sermons.[62] He incorporated it into his theology of the cross. In the framework of our investigation it suffices to note that he did not always use the two terms in the sense they have with Augustine, but sometimes took the words in a more modern sense. *Sacramentum* alone signified an efficacious sign, and thus corresponded to the medieval meaning of "sacrament." *Exemplum* referred to Christ as the model that man has to imitate. In Augustine's usage both words expressed, though in different modes, the notions of efficacious sign *and* of model for imitation or assimilation. One instance of Luther's reinterpretation, from his lecture on Heb. 2, 3, will be considered below, Chapter II, Section 1. Even in the reinterpreted form, the two terms remained an expression of a Christocentric personalism, grounded in grace and practiced in faith and loving imitation of the example.

However, after the consolidation of Luther's new conception of faith the conjunction of *sacramentum* and *exemplum* underwent a significant change. The starting-point of the change is the reinterpretation noted above. But sacramentum has been replaced by "gift" (*donum*).[63] This word stresses the connotation of *possession*. The gift that is Christ is appropriated by reflexive, apprehensive faith, so that if a man believes so, Christ is his own and all that is Christ's is his. Luther stresses that Christ's being a gift is much more important than his being an example. As an example, Christ does not differ from saints, but he is unique by being a gift.[64] Thus the notions, once closely combined, of *sacramentum* and *exemplum*, are now sharply separated, and the *sacramentum* has been transformed into something manageable by the believer, that is, into a gift which he can always "seize" by his faith.

The 1531-35 *Commentary on Galatians* then goes as far as to establish a downright antithesis. Luther starts here from a situation typical of his later spirituality (cf. below, Chapter VI, Section 1). Satan terrifies man by reminding him of threatening words of Christ recorded in the Gospels (e.g. Lk. 13, 25 ff; Jn. 3, 18). In such a situation, Luther teaches, I have to "seize" (*apprehendere*) Christ as a "gift," as him who has fulfilled the law and has died for me. Only "in the day of joy," when I am free from terrors of conscience, may I think of Christ as an example.[65] It is noteworthy that in this context Luther attacks sectarians — the Anabaptists — denouncing as devilish the way they taught Christians "to follow Christ and carry the cross." This implies that he is disavowing the very doctrine which he himself once urged when using the terms *sacramentum* and *exemplum* in conjunction! The notion of gift does not here indicate a personal relationship to Christ. Luther uses the "gift" like a thing, when he "opposes" it (*opponere*) to the Devil, who reminds him of Christ's threats. Therefore, if there is something like a personal relationship at all, then it is to the accusing Devil. Moreover, it is significant that precisely in connection with the idea of gift Luther can say that Christ "*serves* me."[66] This again brings out the notion of manageableness, since a servant is a person at the disposal of and controlled by the master who possesses him.

Augustine's doctrine of *sacramentum* and *exemplum* involved an interpenetration of faith with hope and love. The assent of faith provided the basis for spiritual resurrection, love prompted to acts of penance and virtue, and hope reached out for the final assimilation to the theandric "example." Pre-Protestant Luther in the main retained this doctrine, but reflexive spirituality then caused a total transformation. Hope is absorbed by faith, and love is ruled out, because love, the most distinguished interpersonal relationship, consists in a movement that runs precisely counter to that of reflexive faith. The reflex movement of the mind wants to *possess* certitude, identified with salvation, to *hold* it in the ego once for all. As a result, the old combination of *sacramentum* and *exemplum* is turned into an antithesis, and *sacramentum* becomes the "gift."

In itself, the notion of gift need not imply a depersonalization. It reminds us of the language of mysticism, which uses material imagery, particularly expressions of material union, as forceful metaphors to bring out the intimate union of love. Other elements of Luther's language belong to the same kind. For instance, he can say that "faith has Christ present and included in the heart like a gem in a ring"[67] and, "We are by faith joined to him so as to be one flesh and blood with him."[68] If such statements once more indicate Luther's affinity to mysticism, the mere word "faith" occurring in them is enough to mark a decisive difference. For this word of course refers to *reflexive* faith, as is quite clear from the contexts. Since this kind of faith ultimately bends back on its own subject, the way it "possesses" its object is entirely other than the kind of "possession" involved in the interior movement of mysticism, which consists in an opening and a surrender of the own self. By playing off the gift against the example and "opposing" it to the Evil One, Luther obtrusively emphasizes a non-personal meaning of his material imagery, which comes to signify a claim on Christ to make sure that Our Lord may be at the believer's disposal for his consolation.

CHAPTER II

From Humility to Opposition

1. A Fateful Misinterpretation

Luther, himself, has designated the theology of his early period as a "theology of the cross."[1] This term fittingly describes the idea that dominated his thinking and teaching in the years from about 1509 till 1518. In the framework of our investigation we can consider the theology of those years only in its contrast to the later conception of faith. This entails restriction to very few aspects and omission also of the interesting question about the sources from which Luther drew his inspiration.

The starting-point or center of the theology of the cross is probably the identification of God's judgment and justice. God humiliates man by judging him through His Word, and man, accepting in faith the humiliation of God's judgment, receives justification, which is justice bestowed on him by God.[2] God's "judgment has been shown to us in the cross of Christ . . .; (therefore) we must undergo a judgment similar to Christ's, being crucified and dying spiritually."[3] The spiritual crucifixion is endured in the humiliations of our human life. These are "the mystical cross of Christ," the altars on which "we are offered to God."[4] Faith is self-surrender to the Word of the cross and therefore

31

qualified by humility and self-abnegation.[5] Far from bending back on the self, such faith "takes our selves and all that is ours away from us and carries it all back to God with praise and thanksgiving."[6] Far from "asserting with certitude" one's own state of grace, it teaches man "that he should inwardly sigh for grace."[7]

How, then, did the reflexive conception of faith arise? We must turn to the interpretation of texts from Luther's early period, to find an answer to this question.

In Luther's *Lectures on Romans,* delivered in 1515-16, there are a few passages which seem to foreshadow the new conception. Alluding to 1 Jn. 3, 20, Luther teaches that when man's conscience condemns him he may be confident of the redemption wrought by Christ.[8] Moreover, he speaks of the unfailing testimony of the Holy Spirit and of the necessity for the believer to have this testimony.[9] But all this remains within the potential scope of Christian mysticism. There is no trace of the idea that, in order to be saved, man must assert with certitude that he *is* saved. Concerning certitude of forgiveness and grace, there are at least six passages in Luther's glosses and scholia on Romans where he expressly states that no one can claim such certitude.[10]

In the spring or summer of 1517, while lecturing on Heb. 2, 3, Luther again referred to Augustine's pair of terms *sacramentum* and *exemplum* (cf. above, Chapter I, Section 4). Here he comments: "The *sacramentum* of the passion of Christ is his death and the remission of sins; the *exemplum* is the imitation of his sufferings (*poenae*). Therefore it is necessary for him who wishes to imitate Christ as an example first to believe firmly that Christ has suffered and died for him as a sacrament."[11] This text deviates from previous references to the two terms by stressing the necessity of appropriating the "sacrament" *by faith*. Thus it seems to come very close to the doctrine of reflexive faith. Still, the crucial borderline has not yet been crossed. The reflex realization of the crucifixion's being *"for me"* is not yet postulated as the condition for justification. What Luther urges, here, is nothing but a vivid awareness of the fact of redemption. Nevertheless, if his words are viewed in the light of what he was going to conceive a few months later, they may be regarded as a preparation or foreshadowing of the new doctrine of faith.

This doctrine actually emerged in a lecture belonging to the same exegetical course on the Epistle to the Hebrews and probably delivered in October, 1517.[12] Luther here comments on a sermon of St. Bernard's.[13] He had referred to the same sermon a year earlier while lecturing on the Epistle to the Romans,[14] but by that time he had not yet evolved the essential features of the new concept. St. Bernard urged the necessity for the believer to have the testimony of the Holy Spirit that his sins are being forgiven (*donantur*) gratuitously, that he gains merits through the Holy Spirit, and that he will attain to eternal life as a gift of God. Luther, in his comment of 1517, gives to these ideas a turn that seems to involve only a slight shift of emphasis. He does not explicitly mention the gratuity of God's gift, though of course he does not intend to deny it. He replaces the testimony of the Holy Spirit (in man's heart) with a testimony of man's *conscience* (through the Holy Spirit). He adds that man must believe most certainly (*certissime*); and for Bernard's present tense he substitutes the present perfect: Bernard said that the sins *are being* forgiven; Luther says that they *have been* forgiven and that grace *has been* imparted. The change of the tense gives stronger emphasis to the fact. The other alterations all imply a turn of attention from God the Holy Spirit to man. St. Bernard wanted to emphasize the necessity of the testimony of the Holy Spirit and the gratuity of God's gifts. For Luther, the essential point was the *certitude of man's conscience*. Accordingly, the gratuity of the gift need not be specially mentioned, and the idea of merit is omitted. The reason for the latter omission may be the fact that works become acceptable to God not by man's being certain that they are so but by God's judgment. It required an addition — which Luther was soon going to make — to the new doctrine to depict the acceptability of man's works as dependent on man's conviction that they are so. For the time being, Luther could dispense with the concept of works when he was propounding his new idea.

The anthropocentric shift comes out still more conspicuously in the consequences that Luther draws from his new idea. Applying this idea to the sacraments, he states that "nobody obtains grace because he receives absolution or Baptism or Holy Communion or Anointing, but because he *believes* that he obtains grace" by receiving the sacraments. Here the decisive point of the theory of reflexive faith is enunciated for the first time, though only with reference to the sacraments: grace is received *by* believing *that* it is received. Faith becomes the prime instrument of the reception of grace, provided it includes the conviction that it *is* this instrument. Consequently, man is obliged to believe in his receiving grace *in order to* receive it.

The new doctrine immediately entails criticism of doctrines and practices of the Church. Luther contends that it is "a most fatal error to say that the sacraments of the New Law are efficacious signs of grace in such a way that they do not require any disposition in the recipient except that he should not obstruct" their efficacy by a mortal sin. Instead, Luther teaches that it is faith and confidence in one's obtaining grace which alone makes a man "pure and worthy" of receiving the sacrament of the Eucharist.[15]

There is a noteworthy inconsistency in Luther's comment on St. Bernard's sermon. Luther first emphasized that the certitude of salvation (which, with a misapplication of 2 Cor. 1, 12, he calls "the testimony of our conscience") is not from ourselves but "our conscience *receives* it" from the Holy Spirit. Then he asserts that grace is not obtained by *reception* of the sacraments but by the firm *belief* that grace is being received. Luther conceals this inconsistency somewhat by the phrasing, since the idea of reception is first signified by a special verb (*accipit*) and then in the second statement it is implied in the passive voice (*absolvitur*, etc.). Moreover, what is received is, in the first case, certitude, but in the second case, grace. But in Luther's thought grace and (reflexive) faith tend to coalesce with the latter becoming identical with certitude of salvation. As early as his lecture on Hebrew 7, he held this: "Faith is already justifying grace."[16] Thus the new theory of faith in the first time Luther taught it exhibited an inchoate stage of the discrepancy which Luther never faced or much less resolved. On the one hand, faith is identical with certitude of salvation and with grace and so is given by God. But on the other hand, man has to develop it in the reflection on the *"for me."*

It is no accident that the occasion on which Luther first set forth his new doctrine was a reflection on a sermon by a great mystic. His predilection for St. Bernard — as also for Tauler and for the book, *Eyn Theologia Deutsch* — once more reveals his affinity to mysticism. What St. Bernard's sermon teaches is mystical experience expounded as a gift of God. Luther shifts the emphasis from the giver of the gift to its recipient. In this way the experience becomes an obligatory norm for every believer and the condition for justification. Since the conception of faith included in Luther's interpretation was going to become the center of Protestant spirituality and theology, we may remark that Protestantism as a spiritual movement originated in a man-oriented transmutation of mysticism or religious experience.

2. Desolation, Consolation, and Despair

Did Luther himself, at least in a certain period of his life, have the experience of certitude he postulated as decisive for man's salvation? The answer to this question is not irrelevant to our appraisal of the impact of his new conception on the subsequent development of his thought.

Certitude of grace involves an intense spiritual consolation. As a matter of fact, Luther in his Protestant period often directly equated certitude with consolation. In the framework of the spriitual life, however, consolation cannot but be a transient state. It has therefore to be considered along with its opposite, with this not being for the sake of a dialectic but owing to the immense distance existing between the condition of human nature and the supernatural reality in which genuine consolation is grounded. Since the distance is bridged over by a dynamic relationship, the situation can become conscious as a tension which is the very opposite of consolation, namely, mystical darkness or desolation.

Such desolation was a familiar experience to Luther in his early period. He willingly accepted it as part of his total surrender to God's will out of love for God. Such love, Luther taught in 1516, demands perfect conformity with the will of God. Otherwise concupiscence cannot be eradicated and the Kingdom of God cannot be attained. The surrender is made perfect in man's hating himself and resigning himself even to suffer the torments of hell, if God so ordain.[17] A vivid description of the mental agony of desolation was given by Luther in the first weeks of 1518 in the *Resolutiones* in which he worked out proofs for his 95 Theses on Indulgences. We will translate, here, the whole passage, because it depicts a feature of Luther's early spirituality characteristically different from psychologically similar events in his later interior life.

After citing Tauler as an authority on the subject, Luther continues, alluding to 2 Cor. 12, 2 and obviously referring to himself:

> "I myself also know a man who has stated that he suffered these punishments several times. Though they last only for a very short time, they are so intense and so infernal that no tongue can say and no pen can describe them and no one who has not experienced them can believe it. They are such that if they were to reach their climax (*si perficerentur*) or last for half an hour or even for one tenth of an hour, man would perish totally and all his bones would be reduced to ashes. Here, God seems horribly wrathful, and like him, every creature. There is no escape, no consolation, neither inwardly nor outwardly, but only the accusation of all. Then man weepingly recites the verse: 'I am driven far from thy sight' (Ps. 31, 22). He does not even dare to say: 'O Lord, rebuke me not in thy anger' (Ps. 6, 1). In this moment — it is astonishing to say this — the soul cannot believe that it will ever be redeemed; it feels only that the punishment has not yet reached its end. It is eternal, after all, and the soul cannot believe that it is temporal. There remains nothing but the bare longing for help and a frightful sighing. But the soul does not know whom to beg for help. Here the soul is stretched out with Christ so that all its bones can be counted (Ps. 21, 17). There is no recess in it which is not filled with the worst bitterness, with horror, fright, and sadness, and all this is experienced as eternal. An approximative simile would be a ball passing over a straight line. Every point of the line which the ball touches carries the whole ball but does not comprise the whole ball. Similarly the soul, when touched in its apex by the eternal flood, does not feel or drink anything but eternal punishment, though this does not last but passes away again."[18]

This passage would seem to leave no doubt that Luther had an experimental knowledge of spiritual desolation. But the evidence for his having had the opposite kind of experience is less striking. Nevertheless, there are safe indications that not later than early 1518 Luther did know a spiritual experience which he describes as consolation, or peace. In 1516, while lecturing on Romans, he had taught that in this life peace is not felt nor experienced but can only be accepted in faith, and as late as the end of 1517, while lecturing on Hebrews, he had said that "peace is hidden under the Cross and death."[19] In the beginning of 1518, however, he claimed that peace should be the normal result of every sacramental absolution. We will take up the relevant statement on this below, in Chapter V, Section 1. Here it may suffice to note that it is not easily conceivable how a theologian can postulate interior peace or consoling certitude as the normal result of sacramental absolution if he does not know by experience that such a result is at least possible.

Now in the framework of our investigation we have to ask how the origin of Luther's doctrine of reflexive faith was related to his experience. In the first (German) edition of the present book I suggested a solution which I now regard as doubtful. I interpreted that doctrine as the expression of a potentiality which Luther felt was about to be actualized, as the announcement or expectation of an approaching experience. I thought that probably there was one overwhelming and decisive experience of consolation in Luther's life and that this took place in early 1518. In assuming this, I, perhaps, attributed too much importance to Luther's autobiographical account of 1545 where he unmistakably referred to a time in early 1518 when speaking of his experience of an overwhelming joy: "I felt myself simply reborn and I entered paradise whose gates had opened."[20] But we need not interpret this account as historically exact. It seems more probable that Luther experienced consolation more than once and even earlier than 1518. There is a reference to an intense consolation caused by the consciousness of forgiveness of sin already given in his German exposition of the Seven Penitential Psalms, published in March, 1517.

Luther here speaks to God as follows: In cleansing me of my

sins "thou makest a good conscience in me so that I hear thy se-
cret whisper, 'Your sins are forgiven.' Nobody perceives this
except him who is listening to it. Nobody sees it, nobody compre-
hends it. It makes itself heard, and the hearing of it creates a
consoled and joyful conscience and confidence toward God . . .
All faculties of the soul, which the guilty conscience had made
at once weary and contrite, rejoice and are reinvigorated when
the conscience hears the joy of forgiveness."[21] Such meditations
are most probably grounded in an experience of the author.

There may well have been an alternation between consolation
and desolation in Luther's life at least from about the beginning
of 1517. If this is true, we may interpret his enunciation of the
doctrine of reflexive faith in the fall of 1517 as motivated by his
desire to dispense with the disturbing alternation of peace and anguish. The fact of such a desire is evidenced clearly enough by
the treatise which we will analyze in Chapter V, Section 2. The
new doctrine intended to reason away the threat of spiritual anguish and to establish the consolation of certitude as a theological
necessity.

But the new doctrine did not permeate Luther's thinking and
transform his spirituality from one day to the next. There are also
documents which testify to his resolution to accept the alternation
of consolation and desolation as a spiritual exercise imposed by
God. The most remarkable among these is perhaps Luther's German exposition of the *Our Father* which appeared in print in
early April, 1519, but incorporates material dating back from
1517. This tract, which is one of the most mature products of
Luther's pre-Protestant spirituality, is dominated by ideas
emanating from his theology of the cross and the practice of
humility. In the framework of this spirituality Luther here re-
flects on both consolation and desolation. He writes that God
"at times makes man's conscience find consolation and feel a
cheerful confidence in his grace in order that man may be
strengthened by it."[22] This implies that Luther is aware of what
consolation is and that he has discovered the instability of consolation. Here he accepts this instability, not merely as an inevitable fact but as an occasion for spiritual progress: "that God's
will be fulfilled in us and our own will perish in anguish."[23]

Incertitude regarding the remission of sins has no bearing on salvation; on the contrary, it happens that God "forgives all sins wholeheartedly without telling men, nay, he deals with them inwardly and externally in such a way that they think they have a very ungracious God who wants to condemn them temporarily and eternally."[24] The theory of reflexive faith is not mentioned in the exposition of the *Our Father,* although Luther was already defending it by the time he reedited this treatise. In fact, it is intrinsically opposed to the leading ideas of the tract.

The new theory may be interpreted as an outcome of impatience. It strives by arguing to make secure for a person what can only be expected and received as a pure gift from God. Luther was well aware of the danger of his succumbing to impatience. Impatience, in fact, was one of the themes that preoccupied his mind in the years when the new doctrine of faith was gradually pervading his thought, namely in 1518 and 1519. The theme was treated in his exposition of the *Our Father* of 1519 and, in a most moving form, in some passages from this same time or earlier in his second course of lectures on the Psalms. He was aware that impatience is a defect of the spiritual life, and his radicalism drove him to denounce it in the strongest terms. He certainly hits the mark when writing (in 1519 or 1518) that impatience, which he equates with spiritual dejection (*tristitia*) and disturbance, is rooted in an inordinate longing for success (*prospera*), comfort (*jucunda*), joy (*laetitia*), and glory or renown.[25] Finally, he condemns impatience by saying that it amounts to tempting God.[26]

As remedies against spiritual disturbance and desolation Luther in those years recommended prayer for hope,[27] invocation of the name of Our Lord,[28] and faith in God's Word — faith which is a partaking of the Bread that is Christ.[29] In the context of these spiritual exhortations there is no mention of the practice, which Luther was going to enjoin later, of "asserting with certitude" one's own state of grace.

All the more amazing is the fact that there is no indication in the texts that Luther noticed the actual cause of the impatience which he was so strenuously combating. The exposition of the *Our Father* of 1519 does not refer to the new conception of faith, even though it is clearly defined in Luther's *Small Com-*

mentary on Galatians of 1519,[30] and in portions written in 1518 or 1519 of the second course of lectures on the Psalms.[31] In a number of works written in 1519 Luther evolved it further.[32] He passionately strove to develop it into an instrument for securing to himself and others the certitude of being in God's grace.

This led to two results. *First,* the theology of the cross, though not altogether forgotten, gradually ceased to be the center of Luther's spirituality (cf. Chapter V, Section 2). This theology entails the realization that incertitude and desolation are never a sign of condemnation, but can even be an indication of divine visitation and in any case are a precious spiritual exercise. But Luther's new teaching enjoined certitude as the all-important factor. *Second,* impatience, expressing itself without reserve, came to occupy the center for some time, until, by about 1520, the new theory was consolidated and had produced a spirituality of audacity and defiant obstinacy.

An early document of the degenerate spirituality of impatience is a second exposition of the *Our Father* whose first version dates from 1519 and whose final redaction was published in 1520. No trace of the spirituality of humility is left here. The predominant tenor is anxious prayer for preservation of the supplicant from the terror of incertitude and from despair.[33] It is inconceivable that the laymen for whom Luther wrote the tract were suffering such trials. There can be no doubt that he was describing his own troubles. If certitude of salvation, equated with faith, is the means to obtain, or is identical with, salvation, then incertitude must be coterminous with certitude of perdition. But the attempt to keep hold of certitude or peace or consolation is bound to fail. Luther had made a mistake that is fatal to the spiritual life. Thomas Merton, drawing on the wisdom of centuries of Christian spirituality, succinctly depicts the nature of this mistake:

> "If I think that the most important thing in life is a feeling of interior peace, I will be all the more disturbed when I notice that I do not have it. And since I cannot directly produce that feeling in myself whenever I want to, the disturbance will increase with the failure of my efforts. Finally, I will lose my patience by refusing to accept this situation which

I cannot control and so I will let go of the one important reality, union with the will of God, without which true peace is completely impossible."[34]

Luther, as we have seen, knew very well that "the one important reality" is "union with the will of God." Still, he "lost his patience." Thomas Merton, who probably never read Luther, is sketching here an outline of Luther's spiritual development from 1518 to the end of his life.

3. Opposition

Luther, himself, did not discern the fatal implications of his new concept of faith. He was unable to notice that it was this concept which made his spiritual darkness degenerate into the despair of impatience. However, he was a member of the Church, and the Church did tell him that he was making a gross mistake.

On October 31, 1517, Luther had sent letters to his diocesan Bishop and to the Archbishop of Mainz and Magdeburg, enclosing his 95 Theses on Indulgences,[35] which a week or two later he sent to some friends also. In a very short time the Theses found wide circulation. If we consider the stage of development of doctrine in 1517 it must be admitted, and modern research has left no doubt about the fact, that the 95 Theses were completely within the range of subjects open for discussion in the Church. In early 1518, Luther wrote his explanations and proofs of the Theses, the *Resolutiones,* which he sent not only to his more immediate superiors but also to the Pope. A little later, in the spring of 1518, he composed his *Sermon on Penance.*

These writings, along with the 95 Theses, elicited vehement opposition from the part of some theologians, especially of the Dominican Order, who resented Luther's views as threatening the practice of selling indulgences. The Dominicans succeeded in inducing the Papal *Auditor,* Girolamo Ghinucci, to summon Luther to come to Rome. An interrogation was intended with hopes that he could be brought to recant. But then the political situation made a different procedure appear more advisable. Cardinal Cajetan, who was on a political mission in Germany at that time, was **entrusted** with the examination of Luther's case. He was ordered to hear Luther and demand the recantation of him.

This was a turn of events more favorable for Luther than anything that could possibly be expected in the utterly confused situation. Cajetan was one of the most erudite and clear-sighted theologians of his time. Moreover, his spirituality was similar to Luther's pre-Protestant spirituality of humility. Though differing from Luther in his attitude toward philosophy, Cajetan could even oppose the gospel to Aristotle.[36] Unlike other opponents of Luther, whose invectives were, to say the least, irritatingly shallow, Cajetan clearly perceived the point where Luther was really in danger of lapsing into heresy. The Cardinal prepared himself most thoroughly for the hearing. The notes he wrote down while examining Luther's writings are extant. Even a stiff anti-Catholic of our days, scrutinizing these notes, has found that Cajetan "understood Luther well,"[37] and acknowledged an "admirable insight into the essential"[38] as a distinctive feature of the Cardinal's judgment. Cajetan also differed from other theologians in being quite aware that the doctrine of indulgences was far from being settled in all aspects. Therefore, when he met Luther in Augsburg in October, 1518, he picked out only one aspect of that problem. Luther has said in a later letter[39] that this aspect was not of ultimate importance to him and that, had he been tried only for this point, he would have been ready to recant. So we may confine ourselves to noting that this first point at issue ultimately involved a question about the spiritual power of the Church.

A second issue, however, was the decisive one for both Cajetan and Luther. This was Luther's new concept of faith. While preparing himself for the hearing, Cajetan stated briefly Luther's point, namely "that the sacraments bring damnation to the contrite person if he does not believe that he is being absolved." Cajetan's terse comment on this were the prophetical words: "This implies building a new Church (*Hoc enim est novam Ecclesiam construere*)."[40] Luther, in his turn, composed a report on his encounter with Cajetan, known as the *Acta Augustana*. Here he recounts that the Cardinal criticized as "a new and erroneous theology" his view that it was the "indispensable condition" of justification that man "believe with certitude (*certa*

fide) in his being justified, not doubting of his receiving grace."[41]
Thus, Luther's account and Cajetan's preparatory notes perfectly
agree as to what formed the chief issue. Twenty-eight years
later, the Council of Trent declared the doctrine in question to
be heretical, in stating: "If anyone says that a man is absolved
from his sins and justified by his believing with certitude that
he is being absolved and justified; or that no one is really justified unless he believe that he has been justified; and that through
this faith alone justification and absolution are perfected: let
him be anathema."[42] It is necessary today to recall this Canon
of the Council because there are contemporary scholars who
contend that Luther's conception of faith is not contrary to the
Catholic faith, or even assert that the Council of Trent did not
"understand" the German Reformer.

Cajetan spoke to Luther not as a private opponent but in his
official capacity as representative of the Roman Church, which
is the center of unity of the Universal Church. One may describe
it as a stroke of luck, but it was certainly providential, that the
person whom Luther encountered was a Bishop who had pene-
trated his thought more thoroughly than could possibly be expected of anyone else in Rome at that time. Yet Luther, unfortunately, thought that he was bound in conscience to resist
the warning. This is the more amazing as he was here overriding
principles which he himself had often proclaimed with great
emphasis.

About two years earlier, in his *Lectures on Romans,* Luther had
taught that as disciples of the Crucified One, we should take up
his cross and follow Our Lord, "empty ourselves of everything"
and "divest ourselves of self" (*omnibus evacuari, exinanire nos
ipsos*). This entailed "rejoice most if things develop counter to
one's intentions"; "to will against one's own volition, to be wise
against one's own prudence, to connive at a sin in spite of one's
own righteousness, to be ready to hear a foolishness in spite of
one's own wisdom."[43] In the framework of the same spirituality
he had further enjoined the obligation of yielding to superiors and
to saintly men in the Church; to be ready to hear rather than
insist on one's standpoint.[44] These and similar statements up to
about 1517 sound as if Luther was foreseeing what he was asked

to put into practice in Augsburg. Cajetan's exegetical method and his philosophical views were different enough from the outlook of the German Augustinian Ockhamist. Moreover, he may have tried, at least in some parts of the meeting, to intimidate Luther rather than convince him. So the psychological situation in which Luther found himself was anything but pleasant. Nevertheless, it had been just such annoying, irritating, vexing situations which he was envisaging when he had taught his students — and himself — how to behave as disciples of the crucified Lord. Thus we cannot evade the comment that Luther knew exactly what he had to do as a Christian — and failed to do it when the hour of testing came.

And this was not a case of mere heedlessness. About a year before the hearing in Augsburg, Luther had conceived of his new notion of faith. Then, in the writings explaining his 95 Theses, he had further developed the concept. Now reflexive faith, with its insistence on certitude of grace, was intrinsically contrary to the spirituality of the cross, which willingly accepts the trial of darkness. It is therefore no wonder that Luther was becoming hesitant in his insistence on humility. While traveling to Augsburg, he preached a sermon in Weimar on humility. An account of it is extant, written by Luther himself three months later, after the encounter with Cajetan.[45] The way he treats humility contrasts surprisingly with the tenor of his earlier lectures and sermons. *First,* the persons whom he is exhorting to humility are the Bishops. This was surely justified, considering the situation of the Church at that time; still, since his audience was not an assembly of Bishops, it is astonishing that he says nothing about how all members of the Church could practice humility as an ecclesiastical virtue. On the contrary, he warns his hearers to beware of the prelates lest these might lead their flock astray! Thus he is beginning to call upon Christians to offer resistance to their superiors. *Second,* what is more amazing still is the fact that he warns them to take heed of the priests who preach humility. He says that such preaching amounts to sheer hypocrisy and that the preachers of humility mislead people; but he does not make it clear to what course of action they are tempting them. The confusion of Luther's ideas is — here as in other passages of his writings — a sign that something new has begun to catch hold of his mind without his being able to correlate it with his earlier way of thinking. His former thinking had been centered around the ideas of the cross and humility; the new central idea was that of reflexive faith. In the Weimar sermon this idea emerges too, namely in the expression "righteousness of faith." Luther did not succeed in bringing both ideas into a clear relationship to one another; so, for the time being, the ascendancy of the new concept threw the old one into a twilight of doubtfulness.

In section 2 of this chapter we have briefly delineated and in Chapter V, section 2 we will again refer to the dramatic stress caused by the opposition, not noticed by Luther, between his new concept of faith and his earlier theology of the cross. He could not possibly get out of this fatal crisis merely by interior means. He had the option between two courses, both of which entailed external and interior decision. *Either* he could, at last, put into practice, even on the ecclesiastical level, what he had been preaching for years. He could empty his own self and listen to Cajetan's Thomistic "foolishness" in preference to his own pseudo-biblical "wisdom." He could have decided to hear the Church rather than contend for his private opinion. This external self-humiliation would have led him to interior freedom, to liberation from the cramped introversion of his conception of faith. *Or else,* he could have defended his new doctrine, apparently in deference to truth and in defense of his own peace of conscience. Here the result was bound to be a worsening of the interior crisis, and eventually a decline from despair into defiance and obstinacy.

Luther chose the second course. For some time a wild struggle went on in his mind between respect for the Church's authority and assertion of his own position. In his account of his encounter with Cajetan — the *Acta Augustana* — Luther asserted in one and the same sentence that he was ready to, and that he would never yield to admonition. He claimed that he had "clearly apprehended the judgment of God."[46] He was mistaken. What impelled him to fight for his standpoint was not God's Word but his new doctrine. For this doctrine included not merely a theory but also entailed the individual's working out his own vision of the faith. So the very doctrine he was defending implicitly demanded opposition and resistance.

The interior struggle went on for at least a year. As late as 1519, in his second course of lectures on the Psalms, Luther says that all endeavors for a renewal of the Church are doomed to failure if the First Commandment, which enjoins fear of God and humility, is transgressed.[47] In the same year, in his *Small Commentary on Galatians,* he emphasizes that even though the present condition of the Church may be rotten, under no circumstances does charity allow of a breach of unity.[48] But in the meantime he has dropped many of his earlier rules. Humility, patience, submissiveness, readiness to accept instruction are no longer mentioned. But still love ranks so high in Luther's scale of values that he shrinks from the idea of schism. Twelve years later, however, according to the 1535 edition of his *Commentary on Galatians,* Luther can speak the dire words: "Accursed be charity" and, "Accursed be humility" (*maledicta sit caritas, maledicta sit humilitas*),[49] precisely with reference to attempts at restoring the unity of Christians.

There are documents to show that what drove Luther into opposition and resistance was actually the new concept of faith. In letters from the years 1518 and 1519 he expresses the idea that he feels himself unable to change his view of faith because this would amount to apostasy.[50] Thus he regards his private opinion as the very core of Christianity.

Now if the Roman Church wants to tempt him to apostasy then that Church must be anti-Christian. So from December, 1518, onward,[51] Luther gradually evolved the idea that the Pope was the Antichrist.[52] In the years 1520-1522 he developed an idea of "Christian liberty" or "evangelical liberty" which involved the permission, if not the duty, to put down elements of the established order of the Church, as well as many customs of piety.[53] A climax came with his polemical treatise, "Against the Estate, Falsely Called Spiritual, of the Pope and the Bishops," published in 1522. Here he resolutely renounced humility as well as respect for the Church's authority: "I will henceforth no more do you the honor of allowing you . . . to judge my teaching or to interrogate me. For enough of humility has been practiced, now for the third time at Worms, without any success having ensued."[54] Thus Luther represents things as if he condescended to allow himself to be interrogated three times (in Augsburg, 1518; in Altenburg, 1519; and in Worms, 1521), and as if his humility," far from being readiness to accept instruction, had the purpose of converting his opponents to *his* views. Not for a moment does he ask himself whether it could have been *his* error and obstinacy that made the talks fail.

There is abundant evidence that the "certitude" of his reflexive faith was the reason why Luther thought himself at liberty to offer such fierce resistance. We will quote only one instance. In the invective that we have referred to, Luther goes on to state that he is "certain" of his doctrine and that, accordingly, *he* will now judge the Pope and the Bishops. Further, "he who does not accept my doctrine cannot be saved. For it is God's and not mine."[55] The key-word of all his opposition is a sentence in which Luther sounds like a liberal Protestant of the nineteenth or twentieth century. It is found in his second course of lectures on the Psalms, in a passage from 1520: "In matters of faith each Christian is for himself Pope and Church, and nothing may be decreed or kept that could issue in a threat to faith."[56] The sentence shows graphically that reflexive faith can make opposition to the Church appear as a religious duty.

The disturbance caused by the clash between Luther's allegiance to ecclesiastical authority and his new doctrine seemed settled with his decision for external opposition. But the decision left the interior problem unsolved. From about 1520 to the end of his life, Luther's spirituality remained disfigured by the tangle that had been produced by his option for impatience, which involved the decline from spiritual darkness to psychic despair and eventually to a fluctuation between despair and defiance. We will briefly treat this dismal subject in the last chapter of this book.

CHAPTER III

Faith and Holy Scripture

1. The Word of Promise or the Hermeneutic Principle

In urging private judgment, Luther did not intend to encourage
arbitrary adjustments of traditional dogma. On the contrary, he
kept to the decrees of the first Councils in a manner differing
little from Catholic faith. He insisted that the word of Scripture,
being God's revelation, had to be accepted as true throughout and
that Christians had to hold to the christological and trinitarian
dogmas.[1] He was convinced that his "apprehensive faith" presupposed acceptance of the objective truths contained in Scripture
and summarized in the Creed as well as in the ancient dogmas.
Yet the predominant trend of his thought inescapably called for
adjustments of tradition. Thus a process of dissolution began
with the Reformer himself. He "judged" freely not only dogmas
decreed by later Councils but even statements of the New Testament and whole books of the biblical Canon, notably the Epistle
of James and the Apocalypse. Especially his new notion of
"gospel," which we will explain presently, implies a curtailment
of objective Revelation. Later epochs then came to evolve fully
the implications of the new doctrine of faith. Luther had not
yet drawn all consequences that the logic of his new concept

called for. Therefore, a modern Lutheran can find in Luther's allegiance to tradition relics of Catholicism contradictory to the "Reformational conception of the Word of God and of faith."[2] Many Protestants today altogether reject definite and unified doctrine. Luther did not foresee this; he thought that his principles could safeguard the Church.

Luther had taught a "theology of the Word," and a most remarkable one, already, in his pre-Protestant period. After his discovery of the new notion of faith, he remodeled his theology so that it could serve as a guide to certitude of salvation. He dropped or reinterpreted ideas that did not fit with the new central idea.

Describing Luther's doctrine of the relationship between faith and the Word, Paul Althaus pertinently observes: "Not even the earthly person of Jesus or his miracles and the like are the ultimate basis of faith in the Word."[3] Rather, as Luther says, "the Word for itself, without any respect of person, must satisfy the heart, capture and grasp a man so that he, as it were, caught in it, feels how true and right it is, even though all the world and all angels and all princes of hell may speak otherwise, yea, even if God himself speak otherwise."[4] "Each one must for himself believe only because it is God's Word and because he finds in his heart that it is true."[5]

These quotations graphically illustrate the intertwining of subjectivism and objectivism which is so characteristic of Luther. On the one hand, he teaches that the Word has to be believed "because it is God's Word," and he even says that the Word is "God himself,"[6] thus recognizing the Word as an objective reality that man has to face. On the other hand, however, he does not clearly state that it is the Revealer's authority alone which makes the objective revelation credible. For Luther insists that what matters is not concentration on the Divine Person (Christ or the Holy Spirit) who is speaking in the Word but the believer's being engrossed in the Word. In developing the feeling of satisfaction engendered and nourished in him by the Word, the believer may even disregard the Divine Person who has inspired the Word.

It may be noted, by the way, that this idea of an absolute word-relatedness has been radicalized and systematized by the same

existentialists who have formalized Luther's doctrine of reflexivity. They speak of the "word process" or "speech process"
(*Wortgeschehen, Sprachgeschehen*) of faith[7] — apparently in
order to evade insisting on the content of faith.

Luther's explanation of the way the Word produces faith was
certainly dictated by the desire to provide an objective basis
for the doctrine of reflexivity. St. Paul teaches that faith comes
from hearing or preaching, and preaching from the Word of God
(Rom. 10, 17). Now if the essential message of the Word of God
is, "You are saved if you believe that you are so," then this
conviction will be the easier to gain, the more the message "cap-
tures and grasps" the hearer. And since the essential message is
supposed to be just the turn to the believer's self, he will be
diverted if he contemplates the Author of the Word rather than
concentrating on the idea, "I am saved."

But the attempt thus to establish the doctrine of reflexivity on
the basis of Scripture entails a hermeneutic principle specially
adapted to this purpose. This principle is the discrimination between Law and Gospel. The origins of this discrimination date
from Luther's pre-Protestant period.[8] But later on he evolved it
into one of the mainstays of his system, and it has kept this
position in Lutheranism up to the present day. Luther was well
aware that the antithesis of Law and Gospel was not in accordance with Catholic doctrine. So he observed that "under the
Papacy nobody knew what the Gospel was as distinct from the
Law or what the Law was as distinct from the Gospel; for they
have a faith that refers to the Law only."[9] Strictly speaking, the
antithesis does not signify a mere *fact* but an *act,* an act of spiritual
discrimination to be performed anew time and again. Gerhard
Ebeling aptly notes that the differentiation between Law and
Gospel is not "the mere statement of an existing difference" but
the "performance of a discrimination."[10] Thus Ebeling, like
other Lutheran existentialists, virtually confirms the adequacy of
our approach: what matters for Luther is not primarily dogmatic propositions but ways (and, we must add, aberrations) of
religious practice. For Luther, the discriminative act is identical
with the act of faith, as Ebeling rightly explains.[11] Paul Althaus,
summarizing the gist of a great number of Luther texts, describes

the same act by saying that "faith is in a movement from the Law to the Gospel."[12] This movement, which is assertive faith, consists in "placing the Gospel above the Law, nay, in opposing it to the Law."[13] Luther, himself, can say that the Christian's "supreme art" is "to ignore the Law."[14] Opposing the Law, faith apprehends the Gospel and rests in it, asserting the ego's salvation.

But what is the meaning of Gospel? With Luther this word has not the same sense as in Holy Scripture. In the New Testament the word "gospel" denotes the proclamation of the coming Kingdom of God, starting from the call to repentance (Mt. 3, 2. 17) and including the new interpretation of the Law (Mt. 5-7 and many other passages), the admonition to fear God (Apoc. 14, 6f), and even the announcement of the Last Judgment (Rom. 2, 16). Luther's new doctrine, however, singles out one of the contents of the gospel, namely the consoling promise of remission of sin, and he restricts the meaning of the word "gospel" to this promise.[15] Modern existentialist Protestantism has formalized this doctrine, developing it into a peculiar kind of futurism.

Thus, for Luther the Gospel is the Word of Promise, especially the promise of remission of sin. This interpretation is immediately linked to an instruction for spiritual practice.

Faith, according to Luther, is acceptance of the Word of Promise,[16] and this acceptance is the application of the promise to the believer's self. Thus Luther's term "Word of Promise" by implication connotes the reflexivity of faith. The term construes the gospel as already including the reference to each hearer's self so that the hearer does not believe the gospel if he does not "assert with certitude" that he is saved. In this way Luther tries to give an objective foundation to the subjectivism of his doctrine of faith. Unlike the radical subjectivism of the sectarian "enthusiasts," Luther's doctrine binds the believer strictly to rely on the Word, while practicing "apprehensive faith."[17] The believer can appeal to the gospel to vindicate his assertion. The reference to Scripture as an objective authority disposes of the objection that the assertion of one's own forgiveness might be a delusion. Words of Scripture that are apt to support the objection are neutralized by the mental act which opposes the Gospel to the Law and apprehends the Gospel as the object of faith proper.

2. Luther's Arguments from Scripture

The *Acta Augustana*, which Luther composed after his encounter with Cardinal Cajetan, include the most elaborate attempt that Luther made to demonstrate the conformity of his new conception of faith with Scripture. Luther begins[18] with pointing to Rom. 1, 17: "The righteous shall live by faith" and to Rom. 4, 3: "Abraham believed God, and it was reckoned to him as righteousness." These passages merely state that faith is the origin of justification, and Luther does not try to make them say more than this. He then quotes Heb. 11, 6: "Whoever would draw near to God must believe that he exists and that he is a rewarder of those who seek him." In commenting on this verse, Luther does not go beyond stressing that the believer must have faith in God's bestowing grace in general, even in this life,[19] with the believer's case included but not singled out.

Then Luther proceeds to demonstrate the gist of his thesis: "He who desires to receive the sacrament (of penance) must of necessity believe that he will obtain grace."[20] In other words, grace is given *if* the receiver of the sacrament believes *that* it is given, and the gift is given *through* this very belief. Luther argues that this results from Mt. 16, 19, from the sentence: "Whatever you loose on earth shall be loosed in heaven." He comments: "If, then, you go to the sacrament of penance without firmly believing that you are to be absolved in heaven, you are going to judgment and damnation, because you do not believe that Christ spoke the truth in saying, 'Whatever you loose,' etc., and thus you make Christ a liar by your doubt, which is a horrible sin."[21]

This explanation is an instructive example of application of Luther's hermeneutic principle. The Scripture passage is adjusted so as to bring out what Luther calls the word of promise. The passage speaks only of him who "looses" (Luther understands this to refer to sacramental remission of sins) and of the effects produced by this act in heaven, not of the person to whom the act relates. Luther, however, speaks of this person only. That the text presupposes faith, goes without saying; for in the Church all scriptural words require faith, but faith of a different kind from the one taught by Luther. But there is no hint in the text that this presupposed faith is the *instrument of efficacy* of the "loosing" (whether this word refer to remission of sins, as Luther would have it, or have a more comprehensive meaning, which is more probable). Rather, it is the apostle who is the efficient cause of the loosing, for on him Christ confers the power of "binding and loosing" in the passage quoted. In Luther's interpretation, on the contrary, the function of the priest, who in the post-apostolic time takes the place of the apostle, dwindles to insignificance. Instead, the penitent's conviction of receiving the grace of remission now becomes the proximate instrument of the reception of grace. The text says that the apostle's loosing (in later times represented by the priest's absolution) is, as such, efficacious in heaven. In other words, God ratifies, or is operative through, the agency of his minister. Luther simply ignores this content of the text and instead infers from it an idea which it does not convey or indicate, namely the dependence of the reception of grace on the belief in receiving it.

Luther then adduces further texts from the synoptic Gospels, from St. John's Gospel, and from the Epistle of St. James. In addition, he briefly hints at a few other passages. The texts from the Synoptics he apparently regarded as especially strong supports of his position. In discussing them he uses the terms *fides specialis*[22] and *fides particularis*,[23] which signify faith relating to a single case or to a present effect.[24] These terms supply another characteristic of Luther's new conception of faith. When this faith "seizes" salvation or grace (*fides apprehensiva*) by "asserting with certitude" (*certo statuere*) the believer's forgiveness or state of grace or salvation in a reflex movement of the mind (*fides reflexa*), it is referring to a special, single situation (*fides specialis, fides particularis*). Theological existentialism, which rules out all religious realities except momentary events in which an individual's "existence" is involved or engaged, is thus virtually preformed in Luther's conception of faith, which wants to seize salvation by asserting it with reference to an individual person and to a particular situation.

A "special" or "particular" faith, according to Luther, was that of the Canaanite woman to whom Jesus said, "O woman, great is your faith! Be it done for you as you desire' '(Mt. 15, 28), as also that of the centurion of Capernaum, who said to Jesus, "Only say the word, and my servant will be healed" (Mt. 8, 8). Luther refers to the story of the two blind men whom Jesus asked, "Do you believe that I am able to do this?" and who replied, "Yes, Lord," whereupon Jesus "touched their eyes, saying, 'According to your faith be it done to you' " (Mt. 9, 28f). He points to the story of the officer in the royal service to whom Jesus said, "Go, your son will live," and who "believed the word that Jesus had spoken to him" (Jn. 4, 50). He quotes the Lord's words: "I tell you, whatever you ask in prayer, believe that you receive it, and you will" (Mk. 11, 24); and "If you have faith as a grain of mustard seed, you will say to this mountain, 'Move hence to yonder place,' and it will move; and nothing will be impossible to you" (Mt. 17, 20). He adduces the words which Elizabeth spoke to Mary, "Blessed is she who believed that there would be a fulfillment of what was spoken to her from the Lord" (Lk. 1, 45). He cites St. James (1, 5-7): "If any of you lack wisdom, let him ask God . . . But let him ask in faith, with no doubting, for he who doubts . . . must not suppose that" he "will receive anything from the Lord." He mentions that Jesus frequently rebuked his disciples and St. Peter for their weakness of faith, and he points out that in all these cases a "special faith," relating to a "present effect," is meant. Finally, he indicates some examples from the Old Testament, and cites St. Augustine and St. Bernard.

Luther argues that the same kind of faith which is meant in the texts quoted is required for effective reception of the sacrament of penance, namely faith regarding a present effect, which in the case of the sacrament is remission of sins. He contends that in addition to this faith no preparation or disposition must be required of the penitent,[25] and that this kind of faith alone works grace. He who is without such faith will forfeit grace.

At first sight this argumentation looks overwhelming. Yet there is one objection at least which may presently emerge. The effect of the sacrament of penance is remission of sin; but none of the texts cited speaks of remission of sin. Is it admissible, is it in accordance with Scripture, to treat remission of sin in complete analogy to the granting of petitions to which those texts refer? To find an answer to this query, it is helpful to consider passages that do treat of remission of sin. The result is plain: Nowhere in Holy Scripture, neither in the Synoptics, nor in other writings of the New Testament, nor in the Old Testament, can any instance be found of a person obtaining remission of sin because of his firm belief in the sin being forgiven.

The sins of the paralytic of Mt. 9, 2 are forgiven although he and those who have brought him to Jesus seek only his bodily recovery. It is in expectation of this recovery that they have faith in Jesus. Remission of sin is quite outside the range of their hopes. But the trust in the Lord's person makes possible the gift that is infinitely more important than bodily recovery. — The sinful woman of Lk. 7 comes to Jesus and serves him silently in acts expressive of reverence and humility and love and, probably, repentance. There is no word in the text to indicate that she is sure of receiving forgiveness. But Jesus does forgive her sins, "for she loved much"; and the mental attitude expressed by her silent and humble service is interpreted by the Lord as the faith that has saved her. Her faith (v.50) and her love (v.47) are one. — The story of the centurion of Capernaum does not expressly speak of remission of sin. It is, however, relevant to our inquiry that the centurion does not consider himself worthy of inviting Jesus to come to him, and according to St. Luke's version of the story he does not even presume to approach the Lord in person (Lk. 7, 7). There is no trace of the cheerful audacity and bold confidence which, according to Luther's teaching,[26] should characterize true faith. Nevertheless, the centurion is praised by Jesus for his unparalleled faith — a faith full of humility and reverence and trust. — The most important example is, of course, the tax-collector in the parable of Lk. 18, 9ff. He does not even expressly ask for remission of sin. Overwhelmed by shame and fear, he keeps his distance and does not dare to raise his eyes up to heaven. It is inconceivable that he believed, as Luther's doctrine would have it, that his sins were forgiven, in order that they might be forgiven. It is not even said that he was sure that God had heard his prayer, "O God, have mercy on me, sinner that I am," whereas according to Luther's teaching, lack of certitude would be equivalent to certitude of damnation. But the Lord says: "I tell you, this man went down to his house justified rather than the other," namely, the Pharisee.

The result of this inquiry seems devastating to Luther's position. It appears that the texts he adduced have to be interpreted in a different way. The question that Jesus addresses to the blind men (Mt. 9, 28) provides a clue: "Do you believe that I am able to do this?" This means that what is required of those who seek help of the Lord is absolute trust in his Divine Person and acknowledgment, at least implicit, of what he really is. Such trust involves self-abandonment and is therefore incompatible with reflection on one's own self. Realization of one's helplessness disposes to such self-abandonment. People may even be unaware of the real nature of their misery. That does not matter. Our Lord accepts the offering of undeveloped faith, if only it be informed with humility and trust and love, and he bestows on the seeker a gift that he had never thought of, the remission of his sins. This gift establishes a personal relationship between God and man. God can be implored for it and man can receive it, but it can never be attracted by an anticipating, "apprehensive," asserting act of consciousness which misinterprets itself as faith or trust. Man must seek it in fear and trembling, as the tax-collector did; and it is quite natural and by no means objectionable that the justified one should not be certain of his being in God's favor. Luther, himself, had vigorously emphasized this in his pre-Protestant period, before he had conceived of his theory of reflexive faith.[27]

But we must inquire still further into the nature of the faith that the cited passages refer to. The story of the royal officer, Jn. 4, 46-53, seems particularly instructive. For this text speaks of faith twice (a fact not noticed by Luther in his *Acta Augustana*). At first, to the officer's request to heal his son, Jesus answers, "Go, your son will live," whereupon the officer "*believed* the word that Jesus had spoken to him." Luther noted this much only. Then, after the officer has returned home and seen that his son has already recovered, the Evangelist reports that he and all his household "believed," that is, they became believers. Apparently the first act of faith, which believed Jesus capable of performing the miracle, is different from the second, which is more explicit than the first and is grounded on the experience of the miracle. This interpretation seems to receive corroboration from Acts 14, 9. Here the lame man of Lystra "had faith to be made well," that is, he trusted that Paul was capable of working the miracle, whereupon the Apostle cured him. This happened while he listened to St. Paul's preaching, that is, while he was only on the way to becoming a Christian. The initial faith on which the healing depends, in this and other stories, is naturally *fides specialis*. It is not yet the whole of Christian existence, but certainly already a relationship to salvation. Theological existentialism is right in urging it, since the firm personal trust of this faith remains a quickening force even in mature faith, but it is wrong to represent it as the whole of Christian faith. For Christian faith is not merely a chain of momentary acts looking toward the future, but also an abiding state.

But even the instances of initial faith reported in the New Testament do not justify Luther's doctrine. This is borne out, for instance, by the story of the woman who was suffering from a hemorrhage (Mt. 9, 20-22). The inchoate faith, which is by nature and necessarily belief in the possibility of a miracle, appears in this woman in a quite crude form. She wants only to touch the edge of Our Lord's cloak, trusting to be healed by this touch. Rationalists tend to deride such primitive trust, which seems to rely on matter, as being sub-Christian. Jesus, however, recognizes it as personal, salvific faith: "Take heart, daughter, your faith has made you well." Another case in point is the people's faith in the event recorded in Acts 5, 15f: "They even carried out the sick into the streets, and laid them on beds and pallets, that as Peter came by at least his shadow might fall on some of them." The faith meant in these two stories is personal trust, even though it leans on material symbols. The conviction of the medicinal operation of the sacraments, expressed in many liturgical prayers (but disparaged today by some Catholic rationalists), is a legitimate continuation of a kind of faith sanctioned by a number of New Testament passages, as is the hope of being healed at places specially devoted to the veneration of saints. There is no trace in such faith of that bending back on the believer's own self which, according to Luther's theory, should be the salvific element in faith.

We must therefore conclude that Luther has misinterpreted the passages he adduced. He overstrains the instrumentality of trusting faith. Faith is the way to, or the prerequisite of, salvation, but Luther makes it coincide with salvation itself. This becomes possible because he has first identified salvation with the consciousness of being saved or the certitude of salvation, and then he equates this consciousness with faith. This twofold identification is implied in the following words of the 1531-35 *Commentary on Galatians*: "The remission of sin, the justice, the life and the freedom which we have through Christ is certain, ratified and eternal as soon as we believe so."[28] The consciousness of salvation coincides with, or creates, the existence of salvation. Gerhard Ebeling has grasped precisely the intention of the founder of his denomination when he says: "Faith is not the prerequisite of salvation but, being the certitude of salvation, it is itself the very event of salvation."[29]

An examination of the arguments used by Luther to demonstrate his doctrine of reflexive faith from Scripture inclines us therefore to agree with Cardinal Cajetan who told Luther that the passages adduced by him "were not to the point, and misunderstood."[30]

3. Reflexive Faith and the New Testament

In the foregoing inquiry into the conformity of Luther's theory with Scripture, we took the approach suggested by the Reformer's own early attempt to substantiate his doctrine. This entailed reference chiefly to passages of the canonical Gospels. There are, however, other approaches which also have to be taken if the question of the conformity to Scripture is to be more thoroughly examined. We have previously found that the pronoun *"I"* and the possessive adjective *"my"* play a decisive part in Luther's exposition of his doctrine. The question therefore arises as to the function of the first person singular and the corresponding possessive adjective in statements referring to faith in the New Testament. Furthermore, it has to be asked whether there are statements in the New Testament which express a certitude of salvation, and if so, of what nature that certitude is. Such questions

lead us primarily to the Epistles. Finally, it may be interesting
to scrutinize a few cases of explanation of New Testament texts
in support of the new doctrine in Luther's later works.

There are many passages in the New Testament which ever
since Luther's time have been interpreted as expressing individual
certitude of salvation. The grandest of these passages is Rom. 8,
18 and 8, 31-39: "*I* consider that the sufferings of this present
time are not worth comparing with the glory that is to be revealed
to *us* . . . If God is for *us,* who is against *us*? He who did not
spare his own Son but gave him up for *us all,* will he not also
give *us* all things with him? Who shall bring any charge against
God's elect [plural]? It is God who justifies, . . . It is Christ
Jesus, who died, yes, who was raised from the dead . . . , who in-
tercedes for *us.* Who shall separate *us* from the love of Christ?
. . . No, in all these things *we* are more than conquerors through
him who loved *us.* For *I* am sure that neither death nor life . . .
nor anything else in all creation will be able to separate *us* from
the love of God in Christ Jesus *our* Lord."

In this text the plurals *we* and *us* are used with the same consistency as the singulars *I* and *me* all through Luther's works, not
only in the exposition of the Creed in his *Small Catechism.* Only
in two statements of the act of profession ("I consider," "I am
sure") is the singular *I* used, which is quite to the point, since it
is an individual who is speaking. The contents of the profession,
however, are all referred to a plurality (*we, us, us all, our*), not
to an individual ego.

Let us now inquire whether elsewhere in the New Testament
statements about salvation or communion with Christ refer to
an *ego* or to a *we.* The result is that Christ is called "*Our* Lord"
about sixty or more times, beside many cases where he is simply
named "*the* Lord" or "the Lord *of all.*" On the other hand, the
expression "*My* Lord," so dear to Luther, occurs only four times,
namely in Jn. 20, 13. 16. 28 and Phil. 2, 28. These cases are evidently reminiscences of a linguistic habit. In the Semitic language
of the first Christians it was usual to append to the word *lord* a
possessive suffix, which mostly denoted the singular: "*My* lord."
This implied that the speaker acknowledged the person he ad-
dressed as a real master, as a person having authority over him.

Considering this, it appears the more noteworthy that so few traces of this habit have remained in the New Testament, most of whose authors had a Semitic language as their mother tongue. The fact that the early Christians, when speaking of Christ, in most cases deviated from the usage familiar to them, must have a special reason.

The reason is, of course, the same which caused St. Paul to use the plural exclusively when he spoke of men enjoying communion with Christ, as in the hymn quoted above. In the apostolic time — as well as in the later centuries — the consciousness of salvation was universal and therefore entirely comprised within the consciousness of being God's people, to whom Our Lord has promised that no one shall snatch them out of his hand (Jn. 10, 28). The individual's personal relationship to Christ has certainly been an integral and vital constituent of the Christian religion from the very beginning. Yet, in the mind of primitive Christianity as well as in Catholicism, this relationship is inconceivable outside the primary, comprehensive relationship of the Lord to his Mystical Body, to his Bride, to the Community of his People. The individual Christian cannot think of his communion with Christ apart from his membership in that Body or Community. This is reflected in the linguistic usage noted above.

Redemption, in the consciousness of the authors of the New Testament, is universal, its object being the People of God, the Church, even the Universe: "God has taken care of *Israel* his servant," that is to say, he has established his Covenant with his People (Lk. 1, 54, from Is. 41, 8). "He will save his *People* from their sins" (Mt. 1, 21). Jesus Christ "gave himself for *us* to redeem *us*," that is, the whole of God's People (Tit. 2, 14). Christ has "loved the *Church*, and gave himself up for her" (Eph. 5, 25). In Christ "all the fullness of God was pleased to dwell, and through him to reconcile to himself *all things*" (Col. 1, 19f).

Luther has reversed the spiritual order that had prevailed in the Church since the time of the apostles. Consistently, though perhaps not deliberately, he has transposed the biblical plural expressions into singular ones. Thus, under Luther's pen, St. Paul's words, "If God is for *us,* who is against *us*?" (Rom. 8, 31) become: "If God is for *me,* who can be against *me*?"[31]

Crucial to Luther's religion and theology is his interpretation of the *"for me"* of Gal. 2, 20, where St. Paul says that Christ "gave himself *for me."* The 1531-35 *Commentary on Galatians* admonishes, "Read therefore with great emphasis these words *me, for me,* and make it a habit to apply this *for me* to yourself and not to doubt that you are one of those who are meant by the word *me."*[32] This exegesis is questionable from two points of view. First, modern research has revealed that St. Paul often uses the pronoun of the first person singular not strictly with reference to his own self but in a general or typical sense. Now the Apostle, without any perceptible reason, turns from the plural *we* of Gal. 2, 15-17 to the singular *I* in vv. 18-21. It is therefore most probable that this singular is to be understood in a typical sense.[33] Second, if the passage Gal. 2, 20 is considered in its immediate context as well as in the context of the Apostle's theology, then no doubt can be left that Luther's exegesis is contrary to St. Paul's intentions. The text of Gal. 2, 20 first speaks of a spiritual *death.* In saying, "I have been crucified with Christ," the Apostle professes to imitate the example of Our Lord. Now attention to a personal example that one strives to imitate, and reflex meditation to secure one's own salvation, are two movements of the mind exactly opposite to one another. Therefore, since the text of Gal. 2, 20 conveys the idea of imitation, the words *"for me"* included in it cannot be used as a legitimation for the practice of asserting one's own salvation. On the contrary, this *"for me"* implies that the individual consciousness of the Apostle has in faith been taken up into, or even replaced by, the consciousness of Christ. For the Apostle says: "I have been crucified with Christ; it is no longer I who live, but Christ who lives in me; and the life I now live in the flesh I live by faith in the Son of God, who loved me and gave himself for me." Thus the use of *"for me"* in a typical sense in Gal. 2, 20 is not a mere habit of style but has a spiritual and theological basis.[34] His perfect union with the death and resurrection of Christ enables St. Paul here, for once, to. use the first person singular, though elsewhere communion with Christ is never described in the singular. The Apostle's self "carries the Church within itself and has dilated into an *anima ecclesiastica.*"[35] Thus his certitude of salvation is identical with that of the Church.

The predominance of the idea of sacred community in the consciousness of primitive Christianity is reflected in the fact that the *"for me"* of Gal. 2, 20 is an isolated occurrence. Elsewhere, whenever the New Testament specifies for whom Christ has acquired salvation, the word after the preposition is in the plural: *"for us," "for you," "for all," "for many," "for the Church."* There are more than twenty such cases.

Where Luther retains the biblical plural, he understands it as a singular or he interprets it as signifying a plurality of individuals. For instance, in expounding Gal. 1, 14, a passage speaking of Christ "who gave himself for our sins," the Reformer urges to note the word *"our,"* but adds presently that a man should firmly believe that *he* is *one of those* for whom the Savior sacrificed himself. Thus he uses the plural as a reminder for the individual to realize that *he* is *also* meant, and the individualization is at once turned to practice in exercises in certitude, of which the 1531-35 *Commentary on Galatians* gives copious examples in its exposition of this passage.[36]

The statements of the New Testament on salvation are distorted in their meaning if they are used, as they are continually by Luther, as a basis or legitimation for exercises in asserting the ego's salvation. This practice inevitably dissolves the consciousness of a sacred community which is inseparably and essentially tied up with those statements.

That an assertive spirituality is alien to the New Testament, becomes clearer still if a passage is considered where it is really an individual who speaks of his salvation. At Phil. 3, 12f Paul says: "Not that I have already obtained this or am already perfect . . . I do not consider that I have made it my own." The King James Version translated thus: "I count not myself to have apprehended." This is quite the contrary of *fides apprehensiva.* It is the attitude of humble incertitude which has at all times been the mark of devout Christians. Catholic tradition insists that an individual cannot as a rule claim certitude of salvation unless he has received a special revelation.

Luther, of course, tried to explain this passage from Philippian in accordance with his doctrine. He takes it as biblical evidence to show that, as the *Scholia on Isaiah* say, "even Christians feel the weakness of their faith and are tempted by desolation on account of their sense of sin." The "weakness of faith" according to him consists in the frequent failure of attempts at putting down remorse by exercises in certitude: "It takes a tremendous effort to grasp this by faith so as to be able to believe and say, 'I have sinned and yet not sinned,' so that the conscience . . . may be defeated."[37]

But this is surely not the sense of St. Paul's text. After the words quoted he continues, "But I press on to make it my own, because Christ Jesus has made me his own." This "pressing on" certainly does not consist, as Luther intimates, in exercises of asserting one's own salvation or suppressing the consciousness of sin, but in the fulfillment of the apostolic task, which is the proclamation of the gospel, that is, a *work*.

The passage quoted above from the *Scholia on Isaiah* reveals a radical contrariety, nay, the most essential difference, between Luther's practice of asserting and the thought of the New Testament. The contrariety consists in the different attitude toward sin. Luther's certitude of salvation is continually threatened by the consciousness of being a sinner, with the essential feature being self-assertion in opposition to this consciousness in the thought, "I have sinned and yet not sinned." Now the Church of the New Testament age was certainly aware of being threatened by many perils. In Rom. 8, 35-39 St. Paul specifies a great number of threatening forces and entities and of all of them he says that they cannot separate us from Christ's love. Yet one thing is not mentioned, and this is precisely the one that was for Luther the menacing force *par excellence*: sin, or rather the consciousness of having sinned.

The individual in the New Testament cannot "assert with certitude" his own salvation because his final and eternal salvation is also dependent on his *good works,* in which he has to actualize the grace he has received. In the case of St. Paul, the work required of him is primarily his missionary activity (see, for instance, 1 Cor. 9, 16). He admonishes the Galatians not to be mistaken about the fact that their ultimate destiny will also depend on their works. "Works of the flesh," which are all sorts of sin, will produce "corruption," but works done under the guidance of the Spirit, which are exactly what the New Testament means by good works, will bear as their fruit "eternal life" (Gal. 5, 18-23; 6, 7-10). As the works are an abiding task, there remains an uncertainty with regard to eternal salvation. Certitude would here amount to presumption.

According to 2 Pet. 1, 5-10, it is by works that we have "to confirm" (or: to make safe against loss) our "call and election." Luther, however, thought he could adapt this passage to his system too. In 2 Pet. 1, 9, the man is censured who "has forgotten that he was cleansed from his old sins." Luther claims that this refers to "ingratitude toward the baptism received" and "to the sin of infidelity."[38] But he ignores the context, which leaves no doubt that those who have "forgotten" their baptism are people who fail to do works corresponding to the baptismal cleansing or grace, i.e. works deriving from faith such as self-control, patience, piety, charity. Loss of faith is not envisaged. Rather, v. 1 presupposes that the recipients of the Epistle are faithful. In other writings, Luther offers the explanation that the good works mentioned in the Epistle are a test of (reflexive) faith. He thinks that if a man finds himself doing good works he may take this as a token of his faith being right, since true faith must actuate a man to do good works. Thus, he may once more assert God's favor toward him when he observes himself doing good works.[39] The confirmation of election of which the text speaks would thus depend on a person's asserting the goodness of his works and consequently their and his being agreeable to God.[40] But it goes without saying that this anthropocentric theology misses the sense of the text on which it claims to be based.

According to the New Testament, incertitude of salvation arises not from a man's conscience reproaching him for his sins, but from the conviction that the actions of the justified man, who has obtained the grace of being guided by the Holy Spirit, will be judged. Thus it is uncertain whether he will persevere till the end in faith and love, actualized in good works. Therefore, incertitude is an incentive, not to be stifled by asserting one's own salvation, which urges one to "confirm" the gift of grace by doing good works with "all diligence" (2 Pet. 1, 5), with "fear and trembling" (Phil. 2, 12). The same idea is at the bottom of all exhortations in the Epistles. Because Paul is "apprehended" by Christ, he must "press on" to reach the goal; because it is God, himself, who in the Philippians "works both the will and the deed," they must "work out their own salvation in fear and trembling" (Phil. 3, 12f; 2, 12f).

The relationship between the community's consciousness of salvation and the individual's zeal for self-sanctification is brought out clearly in the First Epistle of John (3, 2f). The community's certitude is expressed in the words: "*We* know that, when He appears, *we* shall be like Him." Then, the necessity for self-sanctification is emphasized, and it is significant that the text here uses the singular: "Every one who thus hopes in Him purifies himself, as He is pure." So the individual's certitude is one of *hope,* which is not absolute because its fulfillment depends on man's self-sanctification, too, but is confident because it is comprised in the absolute certitude that the community as a whole will attain the goal which in later theology is described as the beatific vision.

A special case is 2 Tim. 4, 7f. Here, for once, an individual says that he is certain of his salvation: "Henceforth there is laid up for me the crown of righteousness, which the Lord, the righteous judge, will award to me on that Day." But it has to be borne in mind that the speaker of these words has reached the end of his earthly career. He is awaiting martyrdom in the near future. He cannot work any more. It is therefore an exceptional situation which here makes possible a certitude of salvation. And the ideas associated with this certitude in no way fit in with Luther's system. For the text quoted is preceded by the words: "I have fought the good fight, I have finished my course, I have kept the faith." This passage manifests the conviction that it is not faith alone that secures final consummation, as in Luther's doctrine. On the contrary, the "crown of righteousness" is "laid up" not only for the faith which the speaker has "kept" but also for his "good fight," that is to say, for his work. The Apostle's assurance is thus based on the fulfillment of his task, too — which, according to Luther's doctrine, would have to be condemned.

Even the idea of Christ the Judge, which Luther strove to oust from the domain of justifying faith, is included in the author's assurance, which is a firm hope of being rewarded by the Judge.

Luther, however, ventured to adapt even this text to his system. According to a sermon he preached in 1532, "the crown of righteousness expected by the Apostle is not to be interpreted as beatitude, but as the glory and honor which will be conferred on the faithful worker and battler in proportion to his labor in action and suffering."[41] In Luther's words: "Before Thee, I am a sinner. But as I have served the ungrateful world, He will award me the crown. This will not bestow beatitude, but the renown, the glory and the honor will be there."[42] But this is a wrong exegesis. "The crown of righteousness" of which the text speaks *is* the beatitude, and the crown is expected to be awarded on the ground of faith *and works*.

Luther liked to allude to Jas. 2, 19: "You believe that there is one God; you do well. Even the demons believe — and shudder."[43] He took this passage to be a biblical argument for his view that faith which was merely assent to facts was insufficient. But this cannot be the sense. For, first, James does not discountenance belief in facts as Luther does, but approves of it, in accordance with other New Testament texts that describe faith as obedient acknowledgment of the facts of redemption. Also, the text shows that the demons are far from unmoved by their belief in facts; rather, they shudder. The most important point is that the imperfection of the faith censured by St. James is not that the believer does not assert his own salvation — no believer in the New Testament asserts his salvation in order to attain it — but that such faith is not supplemented by works, as the Apostle clearly expresses: "Do you want to be shown, you foolish fellow, that faith apart from works is barren?" (Jas. 2, 20; some manuscripts have "dead," instead of "barren," or "useless"). In this idea James fully agrees with Paul, who says that "the only thing that counts is faith active in love" (Gal. 5, 6).

So whenever Luther tried to demonstrate his theory of faith from Scripture, he could not but twist the texts. That the doctrine of reflexive faith is contrary to Scripture is shown by the strained nature of Luther's arguments. Moreover, such a doctrine, if maintained, obliterates an essential trait of New Testament spiritual life, namely the inclusion of a Christian's consciousness of salvation in the consciousness of belonging to the sacred community of the Church. It was not Scripture that dictated the new doctrine. Instead, Luther used the doctrine as his chief hermeneutic tool in the interpretation of Scripture.

CHAPTER IV

Faith and Love

1. "Love informed by Faith"

Christian charity is primarily love for God (see Mt. 22, 37; Deut. 6, 5). He who does not love his brethren cannot love God (1 Jn. 4, 20); but the criterion showing that one's brotherly love is a Christian attitude is love for God (5, 2). Love for God is love for Christ and its first and foremost actualization is the fullfillment of God's or Christ's commandments (Jn. 14, 15. 21; 1 Jn. 5, 3; 2 Jn. 6). God enjoins other things, also, beside love of one's neighbor. Hence the anthropocentrism of our time is mistaken in maintaining that love of one's neighbor is the only form of love for God. Love for Christ is the prerequisite for pleasing God (Jn. 16, 27); therefore the Apostle can say: "If any one has no love for the Lord, let him be accursed" (1 Cor. 16, 22). To him who loves God Scripture promises a share in glory, eternal life, and in the Kingdom of God, and that Christ will manifest himself to him (1 Cor. 2, 9f; Jas. 1, 12; 2, 5; Jn. 14, 21). We can love God because God loved us first (1 Jn. 4, 10. 19), because "love is of God" (1 Jn. 4, 7), and "because God's love has been poured into our hearts through the Holy Spirit who has been given us" (Rom. 5, 5).

It seems in place to recall these teachings of Holy Scripture in order to give ourselves a standard for assessing the mutations which Luther's notion of faith caused in his theology.

Luther's new conception of faith, if consistently put to practice, changes the whole structure of Christian life in its spiritual,
practical, and theological aspects. Most of all, the idea of love is
affected. Reflexive faith produces a radical shift in the interrela-
tionships between faith, love, freedom, work, and law. For love
and a reflex movement of the mind are directly opposed to each
other. In true love, as in true faith, a man moves away from his
(false) self to find his (true) self. Reflexive faith, on the contrary, returns to the ego.

Since true Christian charity, or love, is primarily directed to
God, it is love for God that is crippled most by the new kind
of faith. Outside of pietistic movements, love for God or Christ
has become widely unknown or is even expressly rejected in
Protestantism. As early as 1518, Luther denied the possibility of
contrition out of love for God.[1] Melanchthon, the first dogmatist
of Lutheranism, contended that a man suffering the accusations
of his own conscience is unable to love God,[2] and this view, laid
down as it is in one of the Confessions of Lutheranism, has come
to share in the authority that these books enjoy. Luther could
say: "Love God in his creatures; he does not will that you love
him in his majesty."[3]

This quotation shows that, though love for God loses its
primacy, brotherly love is urged emphatically. When Luther
speaks of love he almost invariably refers to love of one's neighbor. We shall see, however, that the new orientation of his religion assigned to brotherly love a spiritual function and a theological position quite different from the place it holds in biblical
and Catholic spirituality and doctrine.

Love is not identical with good works, but is necessarily oper-
ative in them. Good or meritorious works are, by definition,
works done out of love for God. Love is infused by the Holy
Spirit, who is the Spirit of freedom. Therefore, the Holy
Spirit, love, freedom, and good works are inseparably interlinked.
Faith is the basis of love.

In his early lectures on Romans and Galatians (1515-16),
Luther expounded these doctrines in perfect conformity with
Holy Scripture and with St. Augustine's treatise, *On the Spirit*

and the Letter. Like Augustine, he emphasized that good works
are done "out of the Spirit of freedom with the sole motive of
love for God. And these can be done only by justified men."[4]
It is love that makes works meritorious.[5] Such works Luther calls
"works of faith," and he explains that if faith justifies without
"works of the law" it does not justify without "the works that
are proper to it."[6] Thus in his pre-Protestant period Luther made
a clear distinction — which he was going to efface in his Protestant period — between good works (or works of faith) and
works of the law. The *Small Commentary on Galatians* (published 1519) adds the idea of freedom. This piece of a theology
of freedom may have been inspired by Luther's experiences of
consolation, which involved interior freedom (see above, Chapter II, Section 2). Faith receives the grace of love; thus man
can fulfill the law in freedom, without constraint, and with
joy (*hilariter*). Works done in such spirit are meritorious.[7] The
idea of reflexive faith, though set forth in the same commentary,
has not yet influenced the doctrine of love and good works. The
doctrine, characteristic of the Protestant Luther, that justification
is wrought "by faith alone" (*sola fide*), is propounded in the
Small Commentary on Galatians also; but its meaning is widely
different from what it came to mean later. Luther says here,
"Faith alone is not sufficient. Yet nevertheless it is faith alone that
justifies; for, if it be real faith, it impetrates the Spirit of Love."
With St. Paul, he stresses that real faith is "faith working through
love."[8]

A radical difference emerges, however, when we turn from
the *Small Commentary* to the 1531-35 *Commentary on Galatians,*
which is based on lectures he delivered in 1531, then edited and
published by one of Luther's students in 1535. The interrelationship between faith, love, works, freedom, and law is entirely
out of gear.

In Gal. 5, 2, St. Paul exhorts: "Stand fast in the freedom for
which Christ has set us free." In 1519 Luther explained this
freedom as manifesting itself in *action* done without constraint
under the guidance of the Spirit of love. The commentary of
1535, however, does not say a word about action and love. Freedom now consists "in our *conscience* being free and joyful, with-

out fear of (God's) future wrath," and it is actualized not in
love operative through works, but in the assertion of God's favor
to the believer. "For who can fully explain what a great thing it
is for a man to be able to assert with certitude that God neither
is, nor ever will be, angry but will, to all eternity, be a propitious
and merciful Father?"[9] After this interpretation the later commentary gives one of the examples, so frequent in it, of how to
practice the asserting of one's own certitude of being in God's
favor. It is an unconscious understatement when the commentary
groans that this asserting is "most difficult." It is not only difficult, but it is bound to result in an effect directly contrary to
the one desired. One can only shudder at seeing an instruction
for this mental toil of Sisyphus given in a comment precisely on
spiritual freedom.

In Rom. 8, 2, St. Paul distinguished between "the law of sin
and death" and "the law of the Spirit of life in Christ Jesus."
Elsewhere he refers to the latter as the "law of Christ" (Gal.
6, 2), or the law that is "spiritual, holy, just and good" (Rom. 7,
41. 12). It is difficult to understand the meaning of the Apostle's
seemingly contradictory statements. Modern exegesis, carefully
appraising the content of Paul's thought on law, has issued in
results[10] that essentially tally with Augustine's teaching, whose
main outlines the Church has recognized as her own doctrine in
the Decree on Justification of the Council of Trent. Luther, as
late as 1519, was in full agreement with Augustine when he wrote
in his *Small Commentary* that the same law which, as "letter," is
"the law of works, of sin, and wrath," is transformed by infused
love (Rom. 5, 5) into "the law of faith, the New Law, the law
of Christ, of the Spirit, of grace which justifies and fulfills everything." It is not the law that is altered, but man is transformed
so that he can fulfill the New Law in freedom.[11]

There are stray occurrences of such ideas even in products of
Luther's Protestant period.[12] But the dominant tenor of his words
on this subject has become entirely different. The 1531-35 *Commentary on Galatians* has scarcely a word to say about the freedom of love in which the Holy Spirit makes the justified person
capable of fulfilling the law. Law and love are now closely combined and sometimes even equated, and faith is put in grim

opposition to them. The later commentary exhorts: "Set aside (*sepone*) law and love for another place and another time and concentrate on the condition of the present case (*status praesentis causae*)." The believer's present condition consists in his finding himself harassed by the "enemies," which are "Sin, Law, Death, Devil, and Hell." "Therefore," Luther says, "I am anxious to be freed from them." He is aware that Christ has "carried in his body" all those "enemies." He finds "no law, work, or love, that could liberate" him from them. The only way out of the distress, he thinks, is "apprehensive faith."[13] At another place, the same commentary teaches, "In the matter of justification, you should speak of the law with the greatest disdain," but "outside of the topic of justification, we should think of the law with reverence," and should "call it holy, just, good, spiritual, divine, etc. Outside of the conscience, we should make it a God; but inside our conscience, it is truly a devil."[14]

Thus the law is holy just when the believer does not feel concerned by it! His sole preoccupation is how to escape from the terror of his pangs of conscience, and he hopes to succeed by assertive, "apprehensive" faith. The practice of this faith entails repression of all thought of law, love, and work. The tool used for this repression is the "word of promise." St. Paul writes: "I through the law died to the law, that I might live to God" (Gal. 2, 19). In 1519, these words inspired Luther with fine comments on the spiritual law of love and freedom. But his later treatment uses them as a peg on which to hang lengthy instructions pointing out how to free one's conscience from remorse and how to attain certitude of salvation.[15] It seems that justification now depends on the success of a psychic repression.

Still, "love and works" are not altogether forgotten. Rather, they are relegated to a time when the believer feels he has "seized (*apprehendere*) Christ in faith." Then "I do good works, love God, offer thanks, practice love of my neighbor. But *this love or these works do not inform or adorn my faith but my faith informs and adorns my love.*"[16]

The last-quoted sentence implicitly polemizes against the Catholic doctrine that the act of faith is perfected by being informed (pervaded or animated) by love.[17] This doctrine is nothing but an expression of a biblical idea. In 1 Cor. 13, 1-3. 7, St. Paul says that all proclamation, all faith and all works are "nothing" without love; for it is love that believes and hopes. At Gal. 5, 6, the Apostle states that what counts "in Christ Jesus" is "faith working through love." In the Johannine writings, also, faith and love form a unity. God loves the disciples of Christ because they have loved Christ and believed that he has come from the Father (Jn. 16, 27). Therefore, Christ remains in his disciples and they remain in him because they keep the faith (1 Jn. 2, 24), *and* because they love Christ (Jn. 17, 26), *and* because they love each other (1 Jn. 4, 12). Accordingly, they fulfill his commandments (1 Jn. 3, 24; Jn. 14, 15). Further he is said to abide in them because they receive the sacrament of the flesh and blood of Christ (Jn. 6, 56), the sacrament of love. Thus faith, love for Christ, brotherly love, good works, and sacramental cult all lead to the same goal, union with Christ. This implies that the ways leading to the goal form an intrinsic unity. And there can be no doubt that within this living unity love holds the highest rank.

Luther has reversed the traditional doctrine. He teaches that it is not love that informs faith but faith that informs love. This formulation seems to have been an outcome of a polemical impulse. Luther has not elaborated it theologically. What he wants to emphasize is that love has no place in acts relevant to justification or in the spiritual life proper. Only after reflexive faith has been properly established can love and works be practiced. Then they are "informed with faith." This doctrine had fatal repercussions in Lutheran spirituality, as well as in doctrine. Let us first consider a comment relating to the spiritual life.

At Gal. 4, 6, St. Paul teaches, "Because you are sons, God has sent the Spirit of his Son into your hearts, crying, 'Abba! Father!'" In commenting on these words in 1519, Luther set forth the doctrine we already referred to: faith receives the Spirit, who infuses love; love then prompts to action, and this combination with active love makes faith justifying.[18] The 1531-35 commentary gives a verbose exposition of the same passage,[19] but there is no hint that what the Spirit infuses is love! The greater part of the exposition deals with certitude. Time and again, Luther urges that the Christian should "state with (absolute) certitude" (*certo* or *certissime statuere*) that he has the Holy Spirit. It is evident that he does *not* have certitude; nevertheless, he thinks he will forfeit salvation unless he snatches at the certitude of having it, with a direct mental grip. And in the pangs of his anguish he imagines he perceives the Holy Spirit crying, "Abba!" The passage shows graphically that the cramped introversion of the asserting of certitude, which Luther misunderstood to be faith, has not "informed" but has stifled love.

Now if faith, instead of being informed with love, has rather to inform love, what is the part that faith has to play in the just man's good works? We have already mentioned Luther's view about man's obligation to assert that his works are pleasing to God (Chapter I, Section 3). Since the act of faith, in his opinion, amounts to performing an assertion, it is consistent that he could say, as he did in his early Protestant period, that the prime good work was faith itself.[20] The assertion of the works' agreeableness to God is the kind of faith that, according to him, is most intimately tied up with the practice of doing good works. For, as we showed above in Chapter I, assertion not merely accompanies, but even constitutes the goodness of, works. So we may comment that in Luther's doctrine it is in its *assertive* aspect that faith is supposed to inform "love and works."

But it need not be demonstrated at length that in this sort of religious practice there can be no question of love, least of all love for God. If a man, in dealing with another person, asserts that his action in relation to the other is pleasing to that person just because of his asserting that it is so, he is not realizing a true interpersonal relationship, and by no means can such behavior claim to be called love.

In Luther's system, however, the practice of assertion and self-reflection has an important place, not only in the doctrine of faith, but also in connection with the topic of love and works. He teaches that if a man finds himself doing good works, he may take this as evidence that his faith is right, since true faith must actuate man to do good works.[21] In a disputation held in 1543, Luther defended this thesis: "Love is a testimony of faith giving us assurance and enabling us to assert with certitude God's favor . . . "[22] Here love is identified with works to the extent that one word — love — denotes both. It goes without saying that the love meant is mere philanthropy, not love for God. After the first reflexive assertion — "I am in God's favor" — man should watch himself, and see whether he is doing good works. If he finds that he is doing such good works, he should take this as an occasion to assert his being in God's favor a second time, in order to strengthen his certitude.[23] Thus even the theology of love, after being reduced to a doctrine of love of one's neighbor, culminates in encouraging the practices of self-reflection and assertion. Brotherly love is urged, but its theological meaning is entirely altered. Even love is not an outgoing movement from, but ultimately a return to, the believer's ego.

Luther was not unaware of the fact that his doctrine was alien to Holy Scripture. He made desperate attempts to reconcile it with the New Testament. It would take a lengthy treatment to discuss his arguments in detail. For our purposes, it may suffice to give a brief summary of what a modern Lutheran, Paul Althaus, has to say about the matter. Althaus has treated Luther's interpretation of the relevant New Testament passages in two appendices of his book, *The Theology of Martin Luther.* He finds that several New Testament texts on love "at first sight presented difficulties to Luther in many respects" and that such texts "involved a problem for Luther in view of the central tenet of his theology."[24] Finally, even Althaus cannot help admitting that Luther's interpretations of those passages are essentially untenable. Unfortunately, the scholar failed to realize that a theological system whose central tenet is at variance with a central theme of the New Testament must for this very reason miss the essential intention of Holy Scripture.

However, not all writings of Luther's present "love informed with faith" with such a gloomy aspect as it has in many passages of the 1531-35 *Commentary* and other works of his later years. Even a Christian who does not adopt the doctrine of reflexivity will agree when Luther says that faith "does not ask whether there are good works to be done; rather, before one asks such questions. it has already done (its works) and is always busy."[25] "From faith springs love and a liking for God, and from love a **free** and cheerful life and willingness to serve one's neighbor gratuitously."[26] The last quotation is from the treatise, *The Freedom of a Christian Man,* written in 1520. Although, even in this work, attentive scrutiny can detect influences of the doctrine of reflexive faith, this doctrine is not conspicuous. The originality of Luther's religious thought and the wealth of his interior life dominate the picture. Even the 1531-35 *Commentary on Galatians* occasionally describes the relationship between faith and works without any reference to a reflexive conception of faith. For instance: "When sin is forgiven and the conscience has been set free from the burden and the sting of sin, the Christian can endure everything easily . . . ; he does and suffers everything willingly."[27] However, the same commentary can also assert precisely the contrary: "The more certain we are of the freedom that Christ has acquired for us" — which means, of course: The firmer our reflexive faith has become —, "the colder and lazier we become in the service of the Word, in prayer, in doing good, in enduring sufferings."[28] Here it becomes most clear that in his instructions for the spiritual life Luther has forgotten the most important thing: love for God. For instead of drawing the conclusion that the fact of spiritual sloth evidences the insufficiency of a faith that is not informed with love, he continues: "If Satan did not vex us inwardly by spiritual temptations" — that is to say, by loss of the certitude of forgiveness —, "and externally by persecutions of our adversaries . . . we would become entirely careless (*securus*), cowardly, and 'unfit for any good deed' (Tit. 1, 16). Thus, in the long run we would lose our knowledge and faith in Christ."[29] Thus, a dualism of good and evil has to keep the spiritual life in motion. Love is ousted from the center of theology and devotion; its place is taken by the Evil One — a weird picture of deranged spirituality.

2. Love, Works, and Merit

The 1538 edition of the *Commentary on Galatians* makes this startling statement: "If the Pope would concede to us that God justifies sinners through Christ by pure grace alone, we would not only hold him up with our hands but even kiss his feet."[30] Now "the Pope" has not only "conceded" this but declared it to be a doctrine of the Church, and not only after Luther's death, in the Council of Trent,[31] but as early as a thousand years before Luther. For in 531 Pope Boniface II, ratifying the decrees of the Second Synod of Orange, acknowledged the main outlines of St. Augustine's doctrine of grace as expounding the faith of the Church, and these decrees do express what Luther asserted "the Pope" was denying.[32]

It is true that the decrees of the Second Synod of Orange had fallen into oblivion during the Middle Ages. The onslaught of the movement started by Luther may have forced the Church to recall her own doctrine on the subject of grace and justification. The merit of having given the impulse for this reinstatement would wholly be Luther's — had he not, in his Protestant period, disfigured the doctrine of justification by his new concept of faith. As his whole theology is centered around the topic of justification, so justification, with him, hinges on his notion of faith. And it is this notion that opens a chasm between Catholicism and Luther's system. Additional divergences are implied by the consequences that emanate from Luther's central concept and which also have a bearing on the doctrine of justification.

The Church urges the obligation that a man *cooperate* with God's grace. Now this cooperation is coterminous with good works, which are actions flowing from love. Therefore, abiding by the biblical view of the interpenetration of the three theological virtues, the Church teaches that faith, hope and charity are bestowed on man in conjunction and that without hope and charity faith cannot lead to eternal life.[33]

In Luther's system, hope is anticipated or absorbed by the certitude which he equated with faith. The distortion of the concept of faith involves a disfigurement of the notion of hope. We need not enter into Luther's conception of hope.

It is love that presented the greatest problem to him. In assessing his polemics, we have to keep in mind that some late medieval nominalists had contended that man could, by his natural powers, love God above all things.[34] Luther was only defending the Catholic position when he opposed this view.[35] But after he had established his new theory of faith, he did not, unfortunately, confine himself to clarifying the doctrine of the Church concerning love as a gift of God.

MOSTAZAFAN FOUNDATION OF NEW YORK
24 WEST 40TH ST., NEW YORK, NY 10018

BOOK DISTRIBUTION PROGRAM'S
LIST OF AVAILABLE COMPLIMENTARY BOOKS

The Glorious Qur'an
Text and Explanatory Translation by: Mohammad M.
Pickthall

The Holy Qur'an
Text, Translation and Commentary by: A. Yusuf Ali

The Qur'an: The First American Version
Translation and Commentary by: Dr. Thomas B. Irving

Nahjul Balagha: Peak of Eloquence
By: Imam Ali Ibn Abu Talib
Translated by: Sayed Ali Reza

Kitab Al-Irshad: The Book of Guidance
By: Shaykh al-Mufid
Translated by I.K.A. Howard

His attack, in his Protestant period, was directed chiefly against the proposition that faith, in order to be justifying, must be informed with love.[36] He argued that this proposition amounts to ascribing justification ultimately to love. Man, however, cannot have perfect love in this life and, consequently, justification would be impossible.

In another argumentation, Luther contends that if love has a part in justification then justification would not be a pure gift of grace but an achievement of man, wrought through the fulfilling of the commandment to love God and one's neighbor. In short, justification would not be effected by grace and faith alone, but by the law, which would be contrary to St. Paul's teaching.

The first argument leaves out of account the fact that, as Luther himself elsewhere admits,[37] even faith — reflexive faith — is often enough too weak to achieve the salvific certitude. So the same objection that Luther leveled against the role of love in justification, could be raised against faith also.

The second argument acknowledges that faith is a gift of God, *donum Dei,* but forgets that the same is true of love. If, however, love is also a gift of God, then work done out of love for God is ultimately a gift of God, too. Moreover, Luther here equates good works — which are works done in the freedom of love — with works of the Law. This involves a capital misinterpretation of the New Testament. Luther himself, in his early career, had understood his Bible better, as we saw above in section 1 of this chapter. Finally, if faith consists, as Luther would have it, in asserting one's own certitude of salvation, then it would be, though on the psychic level, a human achievement no less than any external "work."

A third argument, defended in a disputation of 1543, acknowledges that both faith and love are gifts of God. But, here, love for God is totally left out of consideration, and love of one's neighbor is again included among the works of the Law.[38] Moreover, Luther argues here that love, being directed to human beings only, is prone to contracting acquisitive, "mercenary" habits. He seems to forget that a behavior which includes such habits is not charity, not Christian love at all.

The astounding weakness of, and the variations in, Luther's

arguments indicate that it cannot have been reasoning or sober exegetical effort which caused his stiff opposition to the doctrine that faith, in order to be living faith, must be informed with love. What, then, was the mainspring of his fierce polemics? The following two quotations may suggest an answer to this query. First, the 1531-35 *Commentary on Galatians* says, "The innocence of Christ and his victory . . . cannot be apprehended by the volition of love but (only) by reason which is illuminated by faith."[39] Second, in a disputation in which his students were debating the proposition that faith justifies without love, Luther himself interjected (in German, while the students were skirmishing in Latin): "We must be *certain* that we are holy."[40]

The joint evidence of these two remarks reveals what is borne out by other statements as well, namely that Luther's prime concern was *to have at his disposal* that certitude which he equated with faith and with salvation. Now there is a certitude inherent in a relationship of love also, but this is not manageable by, nor at the disposal of, either of the partners individually, since it resides in the interpersonal relationship. Hence, Luther deems it insufficient. And it is quite to the point when he argues, first, that only what he has apprehended or grasped in a concept is at the disposal of his mind; and, second, that such grasping or gripping can be performed only by the intellect, not by love. It is, therefore, significant that the Latin verb *apprehendere* (to seize, to grasp, to grip) recurs constantly, sometimes in clusters, where the later exposition of Galatians speaks of justification.[41] By concentrating on the "word of promise," Luther hoped to catch hold of the content of that word, that is, his salvation, or even Christ himself. To ensure this effect, he adjusts the word of Scripture so as to include a reference to his own self. Thus his method, though bound always to fail in spiritual practice, is thought out quite consistently on the theoretical level. It is a kind of psychologism, although not sheer subjectivism, since it does rely on the objective word of Scripture.

Luther's view that man is justified by reflexive faith alone entails, as logical consequence, the denial of *merit*. By 1519, he does not yet seem to have carried his new doctrine all the way to this conclusion. In his pre-Protestant period, he fought vigorously against man's *relying on* his own works and against man's deriving from his works *a claim* to God's mercy. For this, Luther surely deserved well of the Church. Later, however, reflexive faith necessitated an almost total rejection of the ideas of merit and reward.

Most instructive in this connection is Luther's greatest systematic treatise, *The Bondage of the Will* (1525). Here he contends that the reward spoken of in Scripture has to be interpreted not as *corresponding to the* value or worth (*dignitas*) of man's merit, but simply as *following* man's deeds. Secondly, he asserts that passages speaking of reward intend to exhort, incite, console, and encourage pious Christians.[42]

The first argument flatly contradicts a number of Scripture passages which expressly say that man will be judged *according to* (Greek *katá*) his works (Mt. 16, 27; Rom. 2, 6; 2 Cor. 11, 15; 2 Tim. 4, 14; 1 Pet. 1, 17; Apoc. 2, 23; 18, 6; 20, 12). The expression "according to one's works" can only mean that the judgment will correspond to the quality, good or bad, of the works. Moreover, there are six passages in the New Testament which exhort Christians "to lay up for themselves treasures in heaven" by doing works of charity (Mt. 6, 20; 19, 21; Mk. 10, 21; Lk. 12, 33; 18, 22; 1 Tim. 6, 18f). Now what should the word "treasures" refer to, if not to something that has a worth or value inherent in it? It must be emphasized that the idea of merit — dropped by Protestantism and, in its wake, by some progressive Catholics today — is an essential part of the New Testament message, whose relinquishment amounts to a serious curtailment of the gospel. Deeply imbued with the spirit of Scripture, St. Augustine has made it clear, and the Church has recognized it as her own doctrine, that "all our good merits are wrought through grace, so that God, in crowning our merits, is crowning nothing but his gifts."[43] The idea of merit is an indispensable expression of the interpersonality of God's dealing with man. In rewarding man's merit, God acknowledges that the goodness of man's deeds flows from the depth of the created person, namely from charity which is primarily directed *to* God because it has been infused *by* God. Luther's suppression of the idea of merit, on the contrary, is but another symptom of the depersonalization wrought by the reflexivity of his faith. If reward did not correspond to the worth of man's deeds but merely followed it, with the goodness of man's deeds remaining God's exclusively, then God would not deal as Person with man as a person. Living interpersonality would be reduced to a dead mechanism. Man would be little different from a lifeless thing — or else the grace God bestows on him would not be a transforming power.

Luther's second argument shows that he tries to make even the idea of reward subservient to his central tenet. He suggests that the biblical passages speaking of reward should not be taken to mean what they actually say. The hearer or reader of Scripture should interpret them as an encouragement or consolation assuring him "that his works are certainly pleasing to God."[44] Thus, even here, what matters for Luther is solely the believer's certitude of being in God's favor. And this again amounts to a depersonalization. Man would fail to respond as a person to God's personal call if he used God's promise to reward good actions as an occasion to assert the agreeableness of his works to God, and if he imagined that his deeds are pleasing to God *if* and *when* he asserts that they are so.

The twofold depersonalization comes close to a denial of an interrelationship between God and man. If God would not estimate man's deeds as done by man but regard them as exclusively His own — that is to say, not as his gifts but as mere deposits — and if man would himself assert what he ought to leave to God's judgment, then both God and man would act each for himself, without having personal regard to each other. On both parts there would be no freedom and no love, no freedom of love.

3. Secularization

On November 24, 1532, Luther preached a sermon on 1 Tim. 1, 5-7: "The aim of the exhortation is charity out of a pure heart and of a good conscience and of faith unfeigned . . . "[45] One of his students, Cruciger, edited the sermon, and Luther acknowledged this edition by saying: "I think he has done it better than I preached it."[46] So we may take the sermon as a reliable account of Luther's ideas and at the same time as a document of the earliest stage of Lutheranism — just the kind of document suitable for the present investigation. Moreover, the sermon has a special significance as it was preached before an audience of princes whom Luther wanted to win for the divisive Reformation.

The sermon includes excellent ideas on brotherly love. The following excerpts may suffice as examples: "God has commanded me to direct my love toward my neighbor and to be kind in my conduct to everybody, no matter whether he be my friend or my enemy, just as our Father in heaven does, who makes the sun rise and shine over both evil and good men, and does good most to those who blaspheme him by day and night and abuse his good gifts." "You say: 'That man is my enemy and does nothing but evil to me.' Well, my friend, he is God's enemy too, offending Him much more than he can ever offend you and me. Yet my love should not cease or get extinct on account of his being unworthy of it." "It is certainly true that a pious man is more pleasing, for everyone likes to keep company with him; and, on the other hand, one shuns people who are wanton and evil. Still, such conduct is dictated by flesh and blood; it is not yet proper Christian love. For a Christian should not base his love on the (external) person as the world's love does, for instance, a young fellow (basing his love) on the beauty of a girl, a miser on money and property, a lord or prince on honor and power. All this is nothing but borrowed love, drawn from and sticking to outward things." Christian charity, on the contrary, "should be love welling up as from a spring, flowing from the interior of the heart." Such love says: "I love you, but not because you are pious or evil; for I draw my love not from your piety, as from an alien source, but from my own wellspring, namely, from the word that has been engrafted in my heart and which is, 'Love your neighbor.' "[47]

To be sure, the sermon, instead of deriving the genuineness of charity from man's love for God, motivates it by "the word engrafted in my heart," thus betraying, even in this context, the introversion that is so characteristic of Luther's practice of faith. Nevertheless, the sermon does bring out a most essential feature of true charity with admirable depth and clarity. It points out that it is God's love that through His commandment and His examples directs us to love each other, irrespective of the worthiness or unworthiness of the person whom we love. This implies that true charity is at the same time a relationship to God.

All the more astounding is the fact that the same sermon then proceeds to speak about love in quite a different strain. We encounter here Luther's antithetical thinking, which we will specially consider in the last chapter of this book. We shall see that the antithetic statements are both elicited and bound into a sort of unity by the practice of reflexive faith.

After recommending charity by describing its nature, the sermon goes on to exhort "that one should not confuse or mix up faith and love, or behavior toward God and behavior toward man."[48] Love or works of charity entail "purity of heart in the exterior life."[49] "Inwardly," however, man is "totally righteous through faith."[50] For it is faith "that seizes Christ."[51] Thus the sermon ultimately brings us back to the ideas of the 1531-35 *Commentary on Galatians.* Man's attitude toward God consists in faith alone, which is, accordingly, the center of all religious practice. As the *Scholia on Isaiah* say: "Christianity is nothing but a perpetual exercise in this point of doctrine, namely to feel that you have no sin although you have sinned, but that your sins hang on Christ."[52] Although this sentence is not Luther's own formulation, it graphically illustrates the kind of faith he was urging. As we have seen, Luther failed to notice, and refused to mind, the Church's warning, that this conception of faith was alien to Christianity.

Holy Scripture does not even teach the primacy of faith, much less reflexive faith, in the practice of the believer's life. Whereas the prohibitions of the decalogue mainly set limits for man's conduct toward God and his neighbor, the positive attitude enjoined by both the Old and New Testaments is love — first love for God and then, as a consequence of this, love of one's neighbor (Lev. 19, 18; Deut. 6, 5; Mt. 22, 37-40; Jn. 13, 34; 1 Jn. 2, 7; 5, 2; and other passages). The very text that our sermon is explaining emphasizes the primacy of love. In saying that love, which "issues from faith," is "the aim of the exhortation," the text clearly indicates that, while faith is the beginning, love is the perfection. It is therefore in glaring contradiction with the expounded text as well as with the whole message of Scripture when the sermon states: "*Faith* is the chief point of doctrine and the highest commandment."[53] To understand this, we must recall that Luther had reinterpreted the First Commandment of the decalogue as enjoining faith, reflexive faith (see above, Chapter I, Section 3) — an interpretation that needs no refutation. There are quite a number of passages in Luther's works where he discriminates this faith against love in striking and sometimes violent terms.

From the time of antiquity the *Song of Songs* has inspired Christian meditation to compare the relation between Christ and the believer's soul to the relation between Bridegroom and Bride. It is clear that this imagery makes sense only if the relationship in question is one of love. Luther, however, as early as 1520, used the terms "bridegroom" and "bride" to describe the relationship of faith.[54] The 1531-35 *Commentary on Galatians* explicitly excludes love from this spiritual connection. Only when the Bridegroom has gone out of his chamber, are servants allowed to perform their duty, and "then only do works and love begin."[55] Thus, love has no part in the soul's essential relationship with Christ.

In 1 Cor. 13, St. Paul exalts love as superior to hope and faith. Luther audaciously reversed this order and taught his students: "Love should endure and suffer, but faith says to itself, 'you should suffer or endure nothing, but rather rule, command, and control.' "[56]

In a sermon, Luther inculcates the discrimination in question with the outburst: "Love should not curse but always bless; faith has power and should always curse. For faith makes you children of God and takes the place of God, but love makes you servants of men and takes the place of a servant."[57]

If, then, Luther's impetuosity could carry him away to the point of associating the practice of cursing with one's being a child of God, it is little wonder that he should speak in similar terms about attempts at restoring unity among Christians. Referring to Protestant sectarians, he stated, "In matters of ceremony love may be judge and master, but not in matters, of faith or promises. Rather, faith shall have lordship over love, and love shall yield to it."[58] In the later Galatians' commentary, reflexive faith not only exercises its privilege of cursing; it curses even the object of its control, love, in the terrible exclamation: "Accursed be love!"[59] This curse springs from the conviction that truth ranks higher than charity and that one must not jeopardize it by urging unity as a requirement of love. Ultimately, this weird idea is an outcome of confusing charity with letting each one have his way, which, in turn, is a consequence of the loss of love for God. It is quite true that the earthly ideal of undisturbed togetherness can endanger a holy zeal for truth. But this ideal is not Christian charity. True charity is grounded in love for God and can therefore never conflict with truth. The ultimate source of both truth and love is God Himself, whose created gifts, being imitations of His essence, can by their very nature never be opposed to one another.

The position of love, in Luther's system, is strictly controlled by reflexive faith. Love is "gratitude" for the grace man has received in faith.[60] The New Testament clearly indicates and the Church teaches explicitly that true faith is permeated with love while according to Luther, love is merely the "sequel" of faith.[61] Love is for him an indication that faith is genuine,[62] and thus is most useful to man because, as we have already noted, it gives him an occasion to assert once again his being in God's favor when he observes himself doing works of charity. The combination of faith and love is, according to Luther, "the incarnation of faith."[63] However, considering all that Luther says about love, we must comment that in this "incarnation" love is the earthly, inferior constituent. All the fine and profound reflections on charity in the works of Luther's Protestant period never modify his theological evaluation which resolutely subordinates love to reflexive faith. Gerhard Ebeling, distilling the essence of Lutheranism in utter purity, aptly remarks that "the possibility of a heavy tension between faith and love" is conceived "on the basis of the doctrine of justification" of the Reformer.[64]

We have seen that the sermon quoted at the beginning of this section relegated love to the domain of "exterior life." The same idea is expressed in other works of Luther's Protestant period. While the Doctor was lecturing on Galatians in 1531, a student noted his dictum: "The faith that believes Christ serves one's neighbor externally (*foris*) in love."[65] The edited version expanded this idea as follows: "Paul represents the whole of the Christian life as consisting in faith and love." Faith is an interior relationship to God; "love or works" are external behavior toward one's neighbor. "In this way, a man is a perfect Christian: internally, through faith directed to God, who does not need our works; externally, in dealing with men, to whom our faith is of no use but who are in need of our love or works."[66] The *Scholia on Isaiah* are still more radical on the point in question: "The interior life" consists in "faith which is bare righteousness before God." "The external life, on the other hand, has to do with men. It consists in . . . loving one's neighbor as one's own self. This (external) life engenders another righteousness, which is righteousness not before God but before men. This is the righteousness of the law, which comes by works; the other is the righteousness of grace, coming by gracious imputation."[67] This passage is of special interest, as it shows that Luther's disciple who edited the *Scholia* understood love not only as belonging to the sphere of the law and works but even as excluded from the domain of grace.

Though Luther in his Protestant period still acknowledged that love is a gift of the Holy Spirit,[68] he placed this gift in a context that is totally alien to the nature of its giver. The Holy Spirit is the Spirit of Love and Freedom; therefore, when a man serves his brother in charity, his act, being inspired by the Holy Spirit, is a *free* giving of his own self. Luther, however, opposing love to the freedom of conscience, misconstrues the serving of love as a servitude: "Christians are free in the spirit but servants in the flesh."[69] The 1535 published version elaborated this dictum from Luther's lecture as follows: "In order to prevent Christians from misusing their freedom, the Apostle imposes on their flesh the servitude of the law of mutual love so that the pious may recall that, though in their conscience they are before God free through Christ from the curse of the law, from sin and death, still they are servants with their bodies."[70] Thus charity, which in the New Testament is a gift of the Spirit, acting in freedom and lasting to eternity, is here associated with bondage and the flesh and indirectly even with a curse and death. This association is, of course, not a doctrinal statement about the nature of love, yet it is inevitable that love should be practically degraded to such a position once reflexive faith has ousted it from the center of spirituality. And it is quite in keeping with this depreciation when Luther says in the same lecture course on Galatians: "Love believes lies, faith believes truth."[71] On this, the elaboration of the later version runs: "Faith believes God and hence it cannot be deceived. Love believes men and hence it is often deceived. Yet the belief of love is so necessary for the present life that without it life in this world would become impossible."[72] This is a downright travesty of St. Paul's hymn to love in 1 Cor. 13. According to St. Paul, love "believes all things" (1 Cor. 13, 7) because it is a perfection reaching into eternity (13, 8-13): Luther — or, with his sanction, the editor of his lectures — perverts love into a method for coping with secular situations, into a practical measure which is indispensable in view of the permanent imperfections of secular life and which thus inevitably includes the readiness even to put up with "believing lies."

The law, according to Luther, has a positive value only for regulating things of this world. If, then, love is indissolubly linked or even coterminous with the law, it must also be confined to this world. Luther was therefore consistent, although in glaring contradiction to the New Testament, when he taught that only "the plenitude of temporal things" was promised to love, while "a spiritual promise," namely "forgiveness of sins," was given to faith alone.[73] Luther seems to have forgotten that if anything abides to eternity in man's evanescent life, it is love or charity, for "love never ends" (1 Cor. 13, 8). He seems to have forgotten that it is love, and primarily love for God, that transforms man's imperfect deeds into "treasures laid up in heaven." He still believes that in the consummation of eternity faith will cease and there will be only love.[74] But he has severed the connection that exists between love in the state of consummation and the love that is practiced in this life.

In summary, the *conception* of reflexive faith entails rejection of the doctrines of "faith informed by love" and of merit. Moreover, it reduces love of one's neighbor to mere philanthropy and to an occasion for asserting one's own state of grace once more. The *practice* of this kind of faith inhibits or cripples love for God and produces, in a man with Luther's sensitive conscience, terrible disturbances of the interior life. Both the doctrine and the practice make for a depersonalization of the relationship between God and man and bring about a *secularization of love,* that is, a view that takes love and work done in love as belonging to this perishable world only.

Catholicism, however, holds that charity stems from eternity and, accordingly, work done in love extends into eternity — as "a treasure laid up in heaven." Therefore charity, and primarily love for God, is the inner sanctuary of truly Catholic life. The sacred and even sacerdotal quality of such life is actualized by the Christian's officiating in that sanctuary, that is, by his doing works of charity. If, on the contrary, the value of charity is confined to this world, if there is no merit and no reward and if faith — devoid of informing love — ultimately returns to the believer's ego, then man's life becomes profane throughout. This secularization has doubtless been the most fateful and far-reaching effect of Luther's innovation. While imagining that he had reëstablished the baptismal priesthood of all the faithful, he actually laicized and even secularized the whole of the Christian life.

In our time, Friedrich Gogarten has proposed the theory that the secularization of modern life was a legitimate outcome of Christian faith. He would be quite correct if Christian faith were that which Luther made of it. In fact, Gogarten makes his point in a consistent and conclusive deduction from Luther's central idea. Like Luther he establishes a sharp distinction between faith and works. Going a step beyond the Reformer, but strictly keeping in line with Luther's thought, Gogarten attributes to faith the special function "of maintaing and preserving all human doing within the limits of its earthly and secular relevance."[75] For works "have to do with what they bring to pass and with nothing else."[76]

Gogarten could write a booklet to answer the question, "What is Christianity?" without devoting more than a few lines to that principle of Christian life which, according to St. Paul (1 Cor. 13, 13) is "the greatest," namely, love. And Gogarten does not fail to note, strictly relying on Luther, that God "does not want to be loved otherwise than in the love of one's neighbor."[77]

Gogarten's reflections explicitly presuppose Luther's Protestant concept of faith and show us the fateful effects that have developed from this concept. It has led to the anthropocentrism which threatens today to devastate the Christian substance of both Protestantism and Catholicism under the pretense of making the faith more acceptable to modern man and to the secular world.

CHAPTER V

The Sacraments and the Church

1. A New Theory of the Sacrament of Penance

In the context of a theological theory, the new conception of faith first emerged in the framework of sacramental theology. This was to some extent occasioned by the ecclesiastical situation of 1517. Pope Leo X had granted indulgences whose proclamation and administration became a matter of most scandalous abuse. In the vicinity of Luther's city of Wittenberg, the preaching of these indulgences began, in 1517. While hearing confessions, Luther came to learn the results which the preaching of indulgences had produced in the minds of penitents. He found that this preaching was threatening true spiritual penance by leading people to place their confidence in the indulgence letters they purchased. However, Luther's theological formation and his spirituality had not provided him with sufficient principles for working out a clear position on the problems involved. But his pastoral concern brought him into theological discussion of a subject which, as he himself repeatedly admitted, was obscure to him in many respects.

From the years 1517 and 1518 a number of writings are extant in which Luther treats the theology of indulgences and related problems concerning the sacrament of Penance. From the point of view of our inquiry these fall into two groups, one encompassing writings that do not mention the new conception of faith,[1] and one in which this concept plays a decisive role. Roughly speaking, in the first group the indulgences are the central theme, whereas some writings of the second group deal exclusively with the sacrament of Penance and some consider both the indulgences and the sacrament. The link connecting both groups is the idea of penance.

In the context of our study, Luther's treatment of the sacrament of Penance is of prime importance. Luther's earliest attempt to establish a theological explanation of this sacrament is found in his *Resolutiones,* the explanations he wrote in the first weeks of 1517 for his 95 Theses. Though the main theme of this work is indulgences, the expositions of Theses 7 and 38 give a theory of the sacrament of Penance.

The 7th Thesis runs as follows: "God forgives no one's sins without at the same time totally humiliating him and submitting him to the priest who is God's vicar." The notion of humiliation occurring here clearly indicates the atmosphere of Luther's theology of the cross. Luther begins his *resolutio* with the remark that all theologians are agreed on the content of this thesis. "However," he continues, "I am still toiling at the task of understanding it (*in ejus intelligentia adhuc laboro*)."[2] Thus Luther begins by describing the theory to follow as an initial and tentative approach. He admits that he has not yet succeeded in coping with the problems connected with the sacrament of Penance. It is therefore no wonder that his presentation is lacking in consistency. But precisely the confusion of his treatment affords an excellent opportunity to study the transition from Luther's earlier spirituality to what we may call his Protestant way of thinking.

The issue he had first to face concerned the relationship of the priest's sacramental absolution to God's forgiveness. Like other problems connected with the sacrament, this issue had not yet been definitively settled, by his time. Several solutions were being debated. One of these, the one that was going to prevail later, had been propounded by St. Thomas Aquinas. It maintained that God alone forgives sins but saw the priest acting as God's instrument in absolving a penitent just as he does in administering other sacraments.[3] Luther did not agree with this position. To understand his standpoint, it will help to recall the position taken by the theologians to whom Luther owed his theological formation, namely Ockham and Gabriel Biel. On the problem in question, these teachers upheld the doctrine of Peter Lombard,[4] who had taught that God forgives the penitent who is contrite out of love for God, with the priest's function being solely "to declare men bound or released" (*ostendendi homines ligatos vel solutos*).[5] This means that the priest's function is not *instrumental* but *declarative*.

Taking his stand on this bipolar schema of contrition and declaration, Luther outlined a new explanation of the sacrament, incorporating elements of his early spirituality as well as his new concept of faith. He begins by pointing to a seeming contradiction.[6] On the one hand, there are a number of biblical passages which signify that "the remission on earth is prior to the forgiveness in heaven," while on the other hand, "if God's grace does not first remit a man's guilt, one could not even desire to be freed of it."

To solve the problem, Luther resorts to his spirituality of the Cross. The anguish and desolation which formed an essential content of that spirituality take the place of contrition in his theory of the sacrament. Luther even expressly describes those psychic states as "true contrition of the heart." He depicts the terror of spiritual desolation by adapting passages from the Old Testament, especially the Psalms, for instance Ps. 38, 3: "There is no soundness in my flesh because of thy indignation." Luther assumes that in the frightening consciousness of his sins man immediately experiences God's wrath and damnation. He writes, "When God begins to justify a man, he first condemns him."[7] But "in this very disturbance salvation begins . . . Here grace is 'infused,' as (the schoolmen) say . . . Yet at that time man is so little aware of his justification that he even thinks he is close to damnation. He is inclined to think that it is not an infusion of grace but an effusion of God's wrath on him . . . He has no peace and no consolation."

Thus grace is being infused and sins are being forgiven pre-

cisely while man feels himself forsaken by God and finds himself
on the verge of despair. Luther is attempting here to utilize as an
element of a theory of sacramental Penance the identification of
judgment and justice which was the core of his theology of the
cross (see above, Chapter II, Section 1). But, he argues, there
must then be some means to rescue man from falling prey to
despair. This means, Luther then explains, is the declaratory function of the priest administering the sacrament of Penance. When
a priest sees a man in such "humility and compunction," he
should "declare him released and thus give him peace of conscience (*solutum pronuntiet ac sic pacem ei conscientiae donet*)."

Thus far Luther's theory is an attempt to fill Lombard's schema
of contrition and declaration with a new content. Luther's reinterpretation amounts to the claim that every penitent should
have two kinds of *experience* which are very close to mystical
events: an experience that may well be described as a night of
the spirit, and an experience of intense peace and consolation. The
first experience is to replace contrition, the second is posited as
the purpose and necessary result of the declaration of forgiveness
by the priest. It is quite inconceivable that this theory was simply
the outcome of theoretical reflection. Here, as elsewhere, Luther
is evidently positing events of his own interior life as a general
norm, i.e. his previous and repeated experience of a sort of night
of the spirit, and his experiences of consolation and peace (cp.
above, Chapter II, Section 2). It is obvious that such an experimental theory cannot claim any validity as an explanation of the
sacrament as such, for experiences are not constitutive of sacraments. Even as a description of the spiritual process of penance,
the theory holds solely in the rare cases of persons of a spiritual
disposition similar to Luther's.

To the penitent's desolation and consolation, with the latter
being mediated by the priest's absolution, Luther then adds, as the
third element of his theory, the penitent's certitude of forgiveness. He demands that the penitent should rely on the word
of absolution spoken by the confessor and "carefully beware lest
he doubt that his sins are forgiven by God."

Luther points out that the penitent's consolation is given in
faith alone, not in "interior experience" (*experientia intus*). Here

we can only observe that mediation through faith does not change the nature of consolation. Consolation is a spiritual experience and so is, in a still higher degree, certitude. A scrutiny of Luther's presentation reveals that he understands faith as *an instrument to secure* consolation and not simply that peace is to be believed but not experienced. For he says that faith in the word of absolution "will produce peace of conscience (*fides enim hujus verbi faciet pacem conscientiae*)." And, for the same reason, he demands a faith that is itself already permeated with an experience, namely with the certitude of receiving grace here and now. This certitude, inherent in the act of faith, is virtually coincident with peace or consolation.

In dealing with sacramental absolution, Luther extols the priest's declaratory function as "a unique comfort for sinners and unhappy consciences." But this function does not become effective unless the penitent believes that it *is* effective on the basis of Christ's promise. "In general," Luther writes, "the remission of guilt does not become certain to us except through the judgment of the priest, and not even through this unless you believe Christ, as he promises, 'Whatever you loose [on earth] shall be loosed in heaven.' "

Now Christ's words, to be sure, require faith, and he who does not believe Christ's promise cannot expect to profit from it. However, as we saw in the preceding chapters, the point is whether the promise actually signifies what Luther would represent it to mean. For Luther, Christ's promise and the priest's declaratory absolution, which form respectively the objective basis and the objective constituent of the sacramental process, are only occasions to bring about the subjective consolation caused by or coincident with the penitent's certitude. And as Luther goes on pondering, the idea becomes dominant that the penitent's certitude of forgiveness is itself the sign or token or even the proximate cause of forgiveness.

The consoling certitude is "faith in the present grace (*fides praesentis gratiae*)." Since the believer had faith even before he came to receive the sacrament, this faith in the present grace is *faith in one's own faith.* Luther expressly demands this by fantastically adapting the words *fides in fidem* of the Vulgate text of Rom. 1, 17, and adding "The baptized one must also *believe that he believed rightly* and so approached [the sacrament]; otherwise he will never have peace."

Most characteristic of Luther's thought structure is the following statement: "As long as we are uncertain of the remission of our guilt, it is no remission at all inasmuch as it is not yet a remission *for us*; rather, man would fall into even worse perdition if the remission did not become certain, because he would not believe that he obtained it." Luther here presupposes that the remission becomes a remission *"for us"* by our conviction that it *is* for us. This reveals that at the bottom of the doctrine of reflexive faith there is an implicit tendency to represent our *consciousness* of religious facts as the condition or ground of their *existence*. This tendency need only be generalized and secularized, and the result will be a transformation of anthropocentric religion into epistemological idealism or spiritual monism. The philosophers of German idealism were certainly right in acknowledging their gratitude to Martin Luther.

Again and again, Luther's *Resolutiones* insist that belief in receiving a spiritual gift is the prerequisite for receiving it: "You do not have something because the Pope gives it, but because you believe that you are receiving it. You have as much as you believe you have, on the ground of Christ's promise." "The remission of sin and the bestowing of grace is not sufficient, but it is also necessary to believe that the sin has been remitted."

In commenting on the 38th of his *Theses on Indulgence,* Luther returns to the subject of the sacrament of Penance.[7] The Thesis runs as follows: "The remission by the Pope and his cooperation is by no means to be despised since, as I have said, it is the declaration of divine forgiveness." The *resolutio* repeats what Luther said in commenting on Thesis 7: the function proper to the ecclesiastical minister is to impart peace to the disturbed sinner by declaring him absolved. The penitent should believe the word of absolution, and "this same faith makes him absolved in all truth." The latter point, namely the instrumentality of faith in the absolution, receives even more emphasis here than it did in the explanation of Thesis 7. For Luther now plays off faith in one's own absolution against contrition. In expounding

Theseis 7 he described spiritual desolation and anguish as "the real contrition of the heart." By the time he has advanced to Thesis 38, the idea of desolation has lost the spiritual depth it had in the exposition of Thesis 7 and Thesis 15 (for the latter, see above, Chapter II, Section 2). It is now no longer a man's "being stretched out" with the crucified Christ,[8] but is simply intense remorse and the terror of God's wrath. On the other hand, contrition, here evidently understood in the traditional sense, is represented as practically superfluous: "Contrition is not so necessary as faith. For the faith in one's absolution obtains incomparably more than the fervor of contrition." "Suppose a man is not, or does not, deem himself sufficiently contrite but nevertheless with perfect confidence believes the absolving priest and trusts that he has been absolved. I hold the opinion with confidence that this very faith makes him absolved in all truth." "If you believe him who said, 'He who believes and is baptized will be saved,' I tell you this faith in his word makes you being baptized in all truth, whatever the state of your contrition may be."

Luther's more shallow idea of desolation, his omission of its equation with contrition, and his depreciation of contrition in favor of reflexive faith are all factors indicating that reflexive faith was gaining increasing ascendancy in his thinking as he wrote his *Resolutiones.* He started by filling the schema of contrition and declaratory absolution with contents that evidently stemmed from his experience, with contrition being reinterpreted as mystical desolation, and declaration receiving the task of imparting consolation. But then reflexive faith gradually tended to minimize the importance of both contrition and declaration, and consolation or peace was postulated as the result not so much of the priest's absolution as of reflexive faith. There are passages where we can already observe an initial stage of the double equation, so characteristic of Luther's doctrine, of faith both with peace or consoling certitude and, as well, with remission of sin or salvation.[9]

From the foregoing it should be clear that, once reflexive faith occupied the center of Luther's theology, a coherent description of the process of penance entailed suppression of his theology of the cross, at least in its previous form. For this theology taught that grace is given precisely in the darkness of desolation, whereas the new doctrine represents the grace of forgiveness as dependent on — or virtually identical with — the certitude of it. Luther did not succeed in resolving this opposition in the *Resolutiones,* though he must have been obscurely conscious of an inconsistency when he began the seventh *resolutio* with the remark about still toiling for a solution. In fact, no amount of reasoning can remove the inconsistency. If grace is already given in darkness, without the penitent's knowing it, then his becoming conscious of it in an act of certitude can only be accidental. If, however, grace is given only if and when the recipient is certain that it is given, then there can be no bestowal of grace prior to the act of certitude.

It is worthy of notice that the contradiction is not between different contents of experience but between such contents and the postulate that one particular kind of experience is imperative and manageable. Desolation, consolation, and even certitude of forgiveness may well be combined in a coherent description of a series of processes in the spiritual life. And no contrariety need be involved in the theory that forgiveness is given in darkness, while the pronouncement of absolution brings consolation. Further, there is no problem in saying that forgiveness can even become the object of a certainty. The point we wish to make is that Luther did not content himself with a merely descriptive theory, but rather strove to *make manageable* the spiritual process leading from desolation to consolation. This tendency, though but obscurely realized, caused him to apportion an ever-increasing importance to reflexive faith in the process that leads to forgiveness. He postulated that the scriptural basis of the sacrament of Penance implicitly required faith in one's own sins being forgiven, and he represented certitude as the essential quality of such faith since it was based on words of Christ, who will certainly fulfill his promise. Thus, he thought he found a means to make certitude of forgiveness, consolation, and remission of sin available to the believer once and for all.

2. The Dissolution of the Theology of the Cross

During nearly two years after completing his *Resolutiones,* Luther attempted several times to sketch out a fresh explanation of the sacrament of Penance. There are considerable variations in these expositions. Two features, however, recur in all of them and these are the trends which we found, already, in comparing *resolutio* 38 with *resolutio* 7: the theology of the cross recedes, while the doctrine of reflexive faith makes greater headway.

Among the early treatments of the sacraments, the *Sermon on Penance,* composed probably in the spring of 1518, is interesting in more than one respect. Formally, it retains the traditional division of the sacrament into contrition (or attrition), confession, and satisfaction. No doctrine, however, is elaborated about satisfaction. Luther confines himself to briefly noting the traditional view, and for particulars he refers to a German sermon he published recently.[10]

In treating contrition, however, he makes a fresh start. The identification of contrition with spiritual anguish, dropped already in *resolutio* 38, is not resumed. A first confusion arises in so far as Luther does not consistently distinguish contrition — or "true interior penitence" — and the means of stirring this up. He disparages contrition (or attrition) roused by or consisting in detestation of one's sins, asserting that this will only lead to further sins, especially hypocrisy. New in the sermon, is the admonition to rouse contrition or penitence by first practicing love of righteousness, which is developed by meditation on the beauty of righteousness, especially on the examples of virtuous men and innocent children. Love of righteousness will then of itself prompt one to hate his sins. "Penance should be sweet (*dulcis*) and from sweetness descend to anger, to hate one's sins."[11] "The question of how to live a good life in the future should preoccupy your thoughts much more than — nay, it should be your sole care instead of — the question about how to break off and hate your previous bad way of life . . . The best penance is a new life."[12] Penance without any respect to precepts and customs, out of a pure love of righteousness, "is what those [theologians] are referring to when they say that contrition performed in charity causes sins to be forgiven."[13]

Thus Luther's reflection seems to have arrived at a logically satisfactory conclusion. Yet he must have dimly felt that his argumentation evaded the problem rather than tackling it. For he presently grasps the nettle once more. The notion of contrition out of love for God seems to have alarmed him somehow — at any rate, it gives his reasoning another turn. He says that talk about contrition stemming from charity is most obscure for him and that he has never understood it.[14]

> There is nobody in the world who has — or there are very few who have — this kind of contrition. And concerning myself I frankly admit that my case is similar (*de me ipso confiteor similia omnino*). And if you would make a true and free confession, leaving aside God, precepts, punishment, and joy, I know you would say: "If there were no God, no hell, to be sure I would scarcely ever repent."[15]

All this seems to indicate that the disquieting idea of love for God has dissipated the serene image of a "sweet" and "pleasant"[16] penance prompted[17] by the contemplation of the beauty of righteousness and innocence. The question now is no longer about the nature of contrition but about how to become contrite, and penance now seems to be anything but a "pleasant" and "sweet" practice. Man is even quite incapable of coping with this arduous task. Accordingly, Luther now recommends prayer for penance:

> 'O God, thou commandest me to repent, but I am so miserable that I feel I neither will nor can do so. Therefore I prostrate myself at thy feet, begging for thy mercy and grace. Make repentant him whom thou commandest to repent.' . . . This prayer . . . will of itself cause God to regard you as truly repentant.[18] True contrition is not from us but from the grace of God.[19] Contrition begins in the penitent [i.e. in the recipient of the sacrament of Penance] but never ceases throughout his life until his death.[20]

Confusion becomes complete in the section where Luther treats confession. At first, he echoes his theology of the cross by remarking that it is man's "humble confession and prayer" which causes all his deeds "to be forgiven and to become meritorious."[21] Soon, however, it is the penitent's faith in his being absolved which alone secures forgiveness, regardless of his contrition: "Believe firmly that you have been absolved and you will truly be absolved, because [Christ] does not lie, whatever may be the state of your contrition."[22]

Thus, the logical structure of the *Sermon on Penance* is no less confused than that of the *Resolutiones* — and in both treatises it is precisely the inconsistencies that enable us to assess the mutations that were taking place in Luther's spiritual life. First, clear definition of concepts is lacking, so that we are left in the dark about the difference between the act of stirring up contrition and contrition itself, about the difference between contrition and penance (*contritio* and *poenitentia*), and about the relationship between love of righteousness and love of God. There are even a number of downright contradictions in the sermon. At the beginning[23] it is love of righteousness that makes a man "worthy of absolution"; at a later place, however, we must infer that love of righteousness is illusory or futile. For the penance or contrition which it is supposed to bring about is described as, for all practical purposes, never occurring. Also, if love of righteousness makes a man worthy of absolution then reflexive faith cannot have that exclusive function which Luther ascribes to it. Further, as long as Luther is evolving his theory of sweet penance he doubtless presupposes that love of righteousness can actually be practiced and he expects that contrition will arise as its by-product. Then, however, after the emergence of the idea of love for God, man has suddenly become incapable of contrition or repentance and as a substitute for it he has to offer to God his prayer for repentance. Again, this prayer eventually becomes irrelevant because it is reflexive faith alone that matters. Moreover, at one place man's humble confession works remission of sins (*confessione et oratione ignoscuntur*), but after a few lines it is reflexive faith that does the whole job.

How to explain this chaos? All becomes clear if we assume that Luther failed to bring order into his ideas for two reasons. First, the basis on which he is striving to build his theory is inadequate. Contemptuously rejecting all contributions of scholastic theology he exclusively relied on his own experience and on his favorite theologoumenon of reflexive faith. Second, the elements that form the basis of his theory are irreconcilable with each other. We will try to show why.

Luther knew the terrible anguish of spiritual desolation, as he testified in *resolutio* 15. Moreover, there are safe indications from which we can infer that after a prolonged period of spiritual darkness he experienced intense consolation. While writing the *Sermon on Penance,* however, he seems to be in a state of suspense. Consolation has ceased. It is significant that the sermon speaks only of certitude, not of consolation. Apparently the possibility of a return of anguish is looming ahead. But something new has happened in Luther's interior life. He used to face spiritual darkness with patience and courage, but now he fears it. According to his constant practice, he represents his own interior situation as a general norm. This enables us to perceive his apprehension in some instructions which the sermon lays down for the spiritual life. Luther here discountenances "hatred of one's sin" as "a contrivance to produce despair and dejection of the mind," and he deprecates meditation on one's own sins as hypocritical and sinful. These statements are the more revealing as they are precisely opposed to doctrines of Luther's theology of the cross, which also described as a norm a stage of his own spirituality. The theology of the cross recommended the very same practices which the Sermon on Penance rejects: consciousness of one's sin and self-accusation.[24]

In *resolutio* 7 Luther equated "true contrition of the heart" with spiritual anguish. But this was just the state which he is seeking to evade while writing the *Sermon on Penance.* So he now devises a type of penance that does not involve any disturbance of equanimity. He interprets penance as consisting in a preoccupation about leading a new life, stimulated by meditation on examples of virtue and innocence.

But the image of sweet penance goes to pieces the moment the idea of love of God enters into Luther's reflection. He frankly admits that he himself does not have contrition out of love for God. And once more it becomes manifest that his former spirituality has broken down. While compunction and confession of one's sins were prominent in Luther's early teaching,[25] he now says that people, himself included, are unable to feel regret at their sins. Rather, "you are still feeling an inclination for your former life."[26]

This implies that at the level of *cognition* Luther is still holding the position that was characteristic of his earlier period. Above all, he is aware of his concupiscence, and he presupposes that others are aware of theirs. But the *spiritual* attitude which he formerly took in view of this awareness seems to be somehow inhibited now. The reason is plainly that he dreads to fall back into anguish. This also accounts for his avowal of his own incapability of being prompted to penance by love for God. For love of God was closely associated with self-accusation in his early spirituality and since he now shrinks from self-accusation, love for God has become unattainable too.

But why does Luther now fear to accept spiritual darkness? After all, he was the very opposite of a spiritual coward. We cannot, of course, expect to obtain a direct answer to our question from him, for the simple reason that he was unable to realize clearly what was happening in his interior life. But there are indications from which we may infer with high probability the nature of the change.

In analyzing his *resolutiones* 7 and 38 we found that Luther was developing the doctrine of reflexive faith into an instrument for ensuring and making manageable to the believer the consoling certitude of forgiveness as well as forgiveness itself once and for all. Now such certitude is naturally threatened by contrition, which involves precisely the contrary of certitude of forgiveness, namely the acknowledgment of being guilty of damnation. Therefore, if it is imperative for the believer to have certitude of forgiveness in order to obtain forgiveness itself, then he must by all means endeavor to avoid contrition as well as attrition. On the other hand, the enthusiasm of consolation, in which contrition is not actualized, cannot last. Luther does not realize this here, as he did in his exposition of the *Our Father* of 1517-19 (see above, Chapter II, Section 2). He is keeping himself in a state of cramped suspense. He tries to maintain certitude of forgiveness by professing himself incapable of wholeheartedly regretting his sins. This initial derangement of his spirituality produces, as a momentary device, the doctrine of sweet penance. Yet contradictory ideas are pressing forward to overthrow the device implicitly within the same sermon where it was set forth. Luther is honest enough to regret his incapability of regret, and he is heedless enough to record his ideas as they crop up in his mind, leaving them in the state of wild contradiction and thus enabling us to trace the changes that the new conception of faith produced in his spirituality and theology. Since the conception of reflexive faith arose outside of theological reflection on the sacrament of Penance, it also outlived the ephemeral constructions Luther devised to cope with a problem that defied all attempted solutions by the method he employed.

3.   Sacraments as Exercises in Certitude

After the *Sermon on Penance* of 1518, Luther composed two other important expositions of the sacrament of Penance. The first is a German treatise which appeared in the beginning of November, 1519, under the title *Sermon on the Sacrament of Penance.* The second is a chapter in the Latin work *The Babylonian Captivity of the Church,* published in October, 1520. This latter work gives a comprehensive critique and reinterpretation of the Church's doctrine of the sacraments from the point of view of reflexive faith and accordingly includes a chapter on the sacrament of Penance. Parallel to these writings are two expositions of the sacrament of Baptism: a German treatise which appeared in November, 1519, under the title *A Sermon on the Holy and Venerable Sacrament of Baptism,* and again a chapter in *The Babylonian Captivity.*

From all these writings Luther's theology of the cross has almost completely disappeared. A deformed remnant of it turns up in a few lines of the *Sermon on the Sacrament of Penance* where Luther says that he is speaking only to persons "who have distressed, restless, erring, terrified consciences." He claims that such people have "true contrition (*Reue*), nay, too much of contrition."[27] Love for God is not mentioned.

The German sermon makes a strange distinction between penance and the sacrament of Penance. To penance, not to the sacrament, Luther here ascribes the traditional division into contrition, confession, and satisfaction. Concerning contrition, he says in passing — expressly with the sole intention of silencing opponents — that "one should with all diligence perform contrition, confession, and good works."[28] But he does not elaborate a doctrine of contrition. Satisfaction now receives the task which the Latin *Sermon on Penance* of 1518 apportioned to contrition: "The best (satisfaction) is never to sin and to do all good to one's neighbor."[29] *The Babylonian Captivity* retains this new interpretation of satisfaction.[30]

The sacrament proper is now divided into absolution, forgiveness, and faith. "And it is on faith that it all hinges in its entirety; faith alone makes the sacraments effect what they signify."[31] Forgiveness or grace is identified with peace or consolation of conscience: "This is what is properly and truly called forgiveness of sin: that the sins a man has committed no longer sting or disquiet him, but his heart has been filled with the cheerful confidence that God has forgiven them for ever and ever." "Peace — that is . . . forgiveness of sin, which certainly follows faith."[32] This indicates that the sacrament has been entirely psychologized. The priest's absolution is neither instrumental to the remission of sin (as St. Thomas teaches), nor properly declaratory of forgiveness (as Luther held in *resolutio* 7, following Lombard and Biel). "The priests . . . are but servants who propose to you Christ's word on which you should dare to rely with a firm faith."[33] The faith meant is of course, as Luther does not tire of repeating, the penitent's belief in his sins being forgiven: faith "which firmly holds that the absolution and the priest's words are true, on the basis of Christ's words, 'Whatever you will loose will be loosed.' "[34] "As much as you believe so much you have."[35]

Thus reflexive faith has at last succeeded in bringing the sacrament entirely under its sway. The priest's "absolution" is to rouse reflexive faith, which is supposed to work forgiveness unfailingly. Since the priest's function has dwindled to this extent, it is consistent that the person who pronounces what Luther now improperly calls "absolution" need not even be a priest. Any layman, even a woman or a child, can render the same service.[36] Contrition and even confession have become quite irrelevant. The Latin *Sermon on Penance* of 1518 urged prayer for repentance, but the German sermon of 1519, instead, recommends prayer for the belief in forgiveness in case a penitent has difficulties in realizing it.[37]

Nevertheless, Luther's "sacrament" is not sheer subjectivism. It still has an objective basis. This consists in the words of Mt. 18, 18, "Whatever you loose on earth shall be loosed in heaven." Luther persistently retains his misinterpretation of this text, which we have pointed out above in Chapter III, Section 2. In view of the fact that there is no word in Holy Scripture from which the concept of reflexive faith may be reasonably deduced, it is interesting to note that Luther here changes the wording of two passages so that they tally with his doctrine. Unlike the biblical Christ, Luther's Christ says to the paralytic of Mt. 9, 2, "My son, *believe; then* your sins are forgiven." Similarly, at Mt. 9, 22 the Reformer makes the Savior say, "*Believe,* my daughter; your faith has made you well."[38]

One inconsistency, though, has still remained. Toward the end of the tract Luther says: "Nonetheless the remission is as true as if God himself pronounced it, no matter whether or not it cling to you through your faith."[39] Thus Luther here, contradicting what he had said before, admits a remnant of the doctrine, expressive of the very nature of the sacraments, that these are effective not because the recipient believes they are so but because Christ bestows them through his minister (*opus operatum*).

The same inconsistency recurs, with still greater emphasis, in the *Sermon on the Holy and Venerable Sacrament of Baptism.* To be sure, the impact of the new conception of faith is heavy on this tract also. But it was Luther's first attempt to explain Baptism, whereas on the sacrament of Penance he had reflected often through nearly two years. It is therefore understandable that the concept of reflexive faith had not yet transformed the doctrine of Baptism in the same measure as with the sacrament of Penance. As regards the latter, we have seen that it took Luther nearly two years and a number of successive attempts to reinterpret its traditional meaning so as to accord with his new doctrine of faith, and yet by the fall of 1519 one inconsistency had still remained. Keeping this in mind, we will not be surprised to find much of the doctrine of *opus operatum* preserved in the sermon on Baptism.

Luther explains the "meaning" of Baptism as death and resurrection: "The sins are drowned in Baptism and righteousness rises in the place of sin."[40] But this does not imply that sin is really deleted. "As far as the meaning or the sign of the sacrament goes, the sins together with the man are already dead and he has risen, and thus the sacrament has been completed. Yet the work of the sacrament has not yet been completed, since death and the resurrection on the last day still remain."[41] Concupiscence, which Luther identifies with sin, remains. Baptism is a covenant with God and the beginning of a course to be pursued throughout man's life in his "dying for sin" and doing good works until he dies.[42]

Still, the most important element in Baptism is faith. In this sermon also "all hinges on faith."[43]

On this point all the four treatises we are here considering are unanimous. *The Babylonian Captivity* differs from the German treatises only by its radicalism and consistency. The influence of reflexive faith here totally pervades and deforms the doctrine of the sacraments. The *Sermon on Baptism* emphasized that Baptism not only "signifies" but also "works" the beginning of death and resurrection.[44] Instead, *The Babylonian Captivity* merely says that Baptism "signifies" death and resurrection. The reality signified by Baptism as such is man's natural death and his resurrection on the last day. Spiritual death and resurrection, on the contrary, is faith: "When we begin to believe, we are at the same time beginning to die to this world and to live for God in the future life, so that *faith* is truly death and resurrection, that is to say, spiritual Baptism."[45] Sacraments are signs to which a "word of promise" demanding faith is "annexed."[46] "Divine promise" and faith are correlated to each other, "and both of them, being correlative, render true and most certain the efficacy of the sacraments."[47] "What the sacraments work they do not by their own virtue but by virtue of faith."[48] "The whole efficacy" of the sacraments "is faith itself, not their being performed."[49] Sacraments are *not* "efficacious signs of grace."[50] "Baptism justifies no one nor is it of use to anyone; instead, what justifies is faith in the word of promise, to which Baptism is added and which fulfills what is signified by Baptism."[51]

If, then, faith in receiving grace is the sole important thing in the sacraments, what is the use of sacramental signs at all? What function can be left to them under the domination of reflexive faith? To find an answer to this question it seems proper first to consider what *The Babylonian Captivity* says about the sacrament of Penance.

This sacrament here seems to have regained a form outwardly similar to the one it had in *resolutio* 7. Its purpose is no longer, as it was in the German sermon, to bestow psychic comfort alone, and its biblical basis is not solely the word of promise of Mt. 18, 18. Rather, the terror of conscience which in the German sermon was a prerequisite for the reception of the sacrament, has now become part of the sacrament itself. Accordingly, "the divine threat" (*comminatio*) is now added to the word of promise as the objective basis of the sacrament. Both threat and promise, however, are related to *faith*. One has to *believe* God's threat with "a faith which, contemplating the immobile truth of God, shakes, terrifies and shatters the conscience and again lifts it up, comforts it and keeps it contrite, so that the truth of the threat is the cause of contrition, and the truth of the promise, if believed, is the cause of solace — and through this faith man merits remission of his sins."[52]

This is the alternation of terror and comfort which was going to become the center of the spirituality taught by the Protestant Luther. It is a degraded and systematized survival of the mystical antithesis of desolation and consolation. Being essentially a succession of psychic events, it has little to do with a truly spiritual process.

Eventually, Luther dropped Penance as a sacrament because he found that "it lacks a visible sign instituted by God and is . . . nothing but a road leading back to Baptism."[53] Nevertheless, he retained the practice of auricular confession and absolution. *The Babylonian Captivity* explains why: "Though private confession, as practiced nowadays, cannot be proved from Scripture, nonetheless it pleases me wonderfully, and it is useful, nay, necessary; and I would not wish that it did not exist. In fact, I am glad that it exists in the Church of Christ, because it is a unique remedy for afflicted consciences. For having laid open our con-

science and having confidentially unveiled our hidden evil to
our brother, we receive from his mouth a word of comfort pronounced by God. If we accept this word in faith, we give peace
to ourselves in the mercy of God, who speaks to us through our
brother."[54]

Thus it might seem that Luther here accepts the doctrine of St.
Thomas, who teaches that the priest acts as God's instrument in
administering the sacrament. But there cannot be any question
here of a really sacramental function of the confessor. The text
quoted shows quite clearly that for Luther private confession is
now nothing but an excellent means to assuage the affliction of
one's conscience and to obtain solace. The word spoken by the
confessor does not in its own right bring about remission. What
it brings about is comfort and, coincident with this, the faith
that the sins are forgiven. The purpose of confession is thus psychological rather than strictly religious or theological. However,
we must keep in mind that for the Protestant Luther the psychic
states of terror and solace have an eminently theological relevance, since he equates solace with the presence of forgiveness
and with grace or salvation.

This enables us to understand why Luther, precisely because
reflexive faith has become the center of his religious life and
his theology, cannot dispense with sacramental signs. For he
sees these as apt to stir up, develop, and maintain the reflex conviction of one's own forgiveness. The very institution of the sacraments, according to Luther, is designed to "call forth" man's
belief in his sins being forgiven:

> "In saying, 'He who believes and is baptized will be saved,'
> [Christ] has roused (*provocavit*) the *faith* of those who are to
> be baptized, so that through this word of promise man be
> certain, if he is baptized and believes, that he will obtain sal-
> vation . . . Similarly, where he says, 'Whatever you will loose,'
> etc., he has roused the *faith* of the penitent, so that through
> this word of promise he be certain, if he is absolved and be-
> lieves, that he will be truly absolved in heaven."[55]

Luther affirms that it is "arduous" and "very difficult" to believe in one's own salvation.[56] Hence it is necessary that "we exercise our faith (*fidem exerceamus*) . . . not doubting that we

are saved,"[57] and "that one accustom himself to believe the forgiveness of sin."[58] And for this purpose, he teaches, sacraments
have been instituted: it is "an efficacious help to one's faith that
he know he is baptized."[59] *"All sacraments have been instituted
to nourish faith (ad fidem alendam)."*[60] In the case of confession
and absolution it is the confessor's words of comfort that
strengthen reflexive faith. In the case of Baptism a man will be
greatly comforted by *recalling* that a sign tied to a divine promise
has been performed on him.[61] Similarly, the Eucharist is also an
exercise in certitude, as we will see in the next section.

Luther repeated the same ideas in later writings. Although in
his controversy against the "enthusiasts" he described the efficacy
of Baptism in more objectivistic terms than he did in *The Babylonian Captivity*, he did not give up the essential components of
this doctrine of the sacraments outlined in 1520. The primary —
or exclusive — function of the sacraments in Lutheranism has
remained to stir up, develop, and maintain reflexive faith.

The idea of "exercise" emerged in the German sermon on
Baptism of 1519 also, but it is interesting to note that the context
is different here from the one where it appears in *The Babylonian
Captivity*. While the latter treatise represents Baptism as an occasion for exercises in certitude, the sermon taught, "You bind
yourself to remain so [as you have been made in Baptism] and
ever more and more to kill your sins as long as you live until you
die. Then God will accept this and exercise you through many
good works and various sufferings, thus doing what you desired
in your Baptism when you wished to get rid of sin, to die, and to
rise again on the last day and thus complete your Baptism."[62]
This idea of a *moral* exercise has receded in *The Babylonian Captivity*. Instead, another thought of the sermon has gained promi-
nence. The sermon urged that man could and should return to
God, after falling into sin, by recalling his Baptism.[63] In *The
Babylonian Captivity* this remembrance of Baptism becomes the
specific exercise to which a person should feel prompted by
Baptism. For "no sin can condemn a man except unbelief alone.
All the other sins are engulfed by faith in an instant, if there returns or remains a faith in the divine promise made to the baptized."[64] Thus the moral exercise has been replaced with an ex-

ercise in certitude — another indication of the increasing impact which the conception of reflexive faith has exerted on the doctrine of the sacraments in the eleven months that elapsed between the publication of the German sermon and the Latin treatise.

There is a peculiar interpetration of subjectivism and objectivism in Luther's doctrine of the sacraments. The one important thing is faith which strives to *guarantee* salvation by *believing* in it. This faith has an objective basis, which is in the first place the word of Scripture. But before being used as word of promise, it has already been interpreted so as to be suitable for that purpose. Only such previous interpretation can establish the correlation, postulated by Luther, between promise and faith, so that "neither can be efficacious without the other."[65] In the second place, faith is based on the sacramental sign which is seen, heard, or remembered. Although this is but an auxiliary basis, reminding the believer of the word of promise, it has a most useful, if not indispensable, function. For the word of promise becomes *perceptible* in the sign tied up with it. As we explained in a previous chapter, the word of promise may be compared with a reflecting surface. From this surface the ray of faith is expected to return to its subject. Now this return is easier and safer if the reflecting surface is not merely thought of but perceived. In a tract on the Eucharist composed in 1520, Luther expresses this in the following words: "We poor men, living on the five senses, must have, besides the words, an external sign to hold fast to."[66] This is why Luther attached such great importance to the sacraments — although, by the same token, sacraments were superfluous for him provided a man had the proper kind of faith. Though subordinated to the word of promise, sacraments are to bring about the one all-important objective of forgiveness, which is grace and salvation.

4. A Reinterpretation of the Eucharist

Luther wrote several treatises on the Eucharist. Three of them are of special importance for our investigation. The first is a German work which appeared in December, 1519, and bears the title *"A Sermon on the Blessed Sacrament of the Holy True Body of Christ . . ."* The second, also in German, is *"A Sermon on the*

New Testament, that is to say, Holy Mass," published in April, 1520. Thirdly, there is a chapter on the Eucharist in *The Babylonian Captivity.* The second and third of these works agree on all essential points. There are enormous differences, however, between the first sermon and the two later works. A comparison of these treatises reveals that in the course of a few months reflexive faith had completely altered Luther's interpretation of the sacrament of the altar.

The sermon of 1519, to be sure, urges reflexive faith: "You must believe that you have obtained it."[67] And Luther also represents the sacrament as an exercise in certitude: "It is necessary and good that you . . . exercise and strengthen such faith while attending Mass."[68] Yet the new conception has not yet substantially changed the doctrine of the sacrament. Luther is largely drawing on the Catholic heritage of eucharistic spirituality. He writes:

"The meaning or purpose of this sacrament is the communion of all the saints."[69] "Just as bread is prepared out of many small grains which become one loaf (or: one body[70]) of bread, with each grain losing its own body and shape and entering into the common body of bread, and just as the grapes, losing their shape, turn into the common beverage of wine — so we also should be, and so we are if we properly use this sacrament. Christ with all saints through his love assumes our shape and fights with us against sin, death and all evil. This enkindles our love so that we assume his form and rely on his righteousness, life and blessedness, and thus, through a fellowship of his riches with our misery, we are one cake, one body (or: loaf), one beverage, and we have everything in common with him. Yes, this is a great sacrament (or: mystery), says St. Paul (Eph. 5, 32), namely, that Christ and the Church are one flesh and bone. Again, we should also allow ourselves to be transformed by this same love, regarding the afflictions of all other Christians as ours, adopting their form and needs as ours, and letting them share in all good things that we can afford so that they may enjoy them. This is proper communion and the true meaning of this sacrament. In this manner we are mutually transformed into each other and establish communion through love, without which no change can occur."

"We become one with Christ and are incorporated into him with all saints, so that he participates in what is ours, acting and forbearing for us as if he were what we are and as if he were affected — nay, he is more affected than we are — by things that affect us. Again, we are allowed to participate in what is his as if we were what he is, and at the end of all things this will come to pass in our becoming like him, as St. John says: 'We know that when he appears we shall be like him' (1 Jn. 3, 2). So deep and thoroughgoing is the communion of Christ and all saints with us."

Ideas similar to these occur in Luther's sermons up to 1524.[71] In accord with the Church's century-long tradition, they bring out forcefully the relation of the Eucharist to the Body of Christ which is the Church.

Gradually, however, a novel doctrine of the Lord's Supper, controlled by reflexive faith, came to supplant such ideas. The change is drastically illustrated, for instance, by the *Scholia on Isaiah* which are based on lectures delivered 1527-29. Here Luther even expressly denies that the Eucharist has something to do with strengthening mutual charity.[72] The new interpretation of the Lord's Supper, which was to dominate later Protestant spirituality, first emerged in Luther's *Sermon of the New Testament* of 1520, and was repeated in the relevant chapter of *The Babylonian Captivity*.

The relation of the Eucharist to the Church as a community, which formed a prominent theme of the 1519 sermon, is not mentioned at all in the chapter on the Eucharist in *The Babylonian Captivity*. The Sermon of 1520 has nothing about this important subject except the thin remark that, in order to promote unity and to prevent schisms, Christ has given but one law to his people, which is Holy Mass.[73] The tenor of both treatises is that of juridical individualism.

This tenor is manifest from the very outset in Luther's interpretation of the word *testamentum*. He does not take this word in the sense of "covenant," which it has in the passage where Christ is speaking of his blood poured out as "my blood of the (New) Testament" (Mt. 26, 28). Instead, Luther claims that it means "the last will" of Christ. This will, he explains, is expressed in the words of institution, which are "the principal part" or the "substance" of the Mass.[74] A testament is "the promise by which a person at the point of death bequeaths his heritage and appoints heirs to it." Christ's last will indicates the bequest by the words "for the remission of sins." The heirs are signified by the words "for you and for many." These, Luther comments, are those "who accept and believe the promise of the testator, for it is faith that here constitutes heirs (*fides enim hic haeredes facit*)."[75]

In this manner Luther manages to reinterpret the Mass as "a promise of remission of sins" to be accepted with reflexive faith. "For man can meet or deal with God in no other way than by faith."[76] Promise and faith in the word of promise constitute the relationship between God and man.[77] To his promise, God has added a pledge or token, much as he used to do in the Old Testament. The pledge or token is the Body and Blood of Christ. Luther has Christ say, "In order that you may be quite certain of this my promise, I will give over (*tradam*) my body and pour out my blood."[78]

There are thus three main constituents of the Mass: Christ's promise, the token attached to the promise, and man's faith in this promise. The words of promise are far more important than the token, and in fact a man can quite well do without the token if he believes the word of promise.[79] "I can . . . at any time have Mass, holding up to myself the words of Christ, nourishing and strengthening my faith on them."[80]

Nevertheless, the pledge or token is most helpful, and is even indispensable in view of the weakness of the human mind. Being Christ's "own true flesh and blood under the bread and wine," it is "a powerful and most noble seal" on the testament, given with a view "to increasing the assurance and strength of our faith."[81] This makes it understandable why Luther so emphatically insisted on the doctrine of the Real Presence. If the Mass is Christ's promise of remission of sins to him who believes that his sins are forgiven, then the bodily presence of the one promising at the time of the proclamation of his promise most surely guarantees the validity of the promise and the actuality of its accomplishment.

A testament entitles the heir to lay a legal claim to his heritage. In the case of the Mass, the claimant is the believer and the assertion of his claim is his faith. In both the Latin and the German treatises Luther expressly ascribes to the believer a "title to the testament" (*jus testamenti, Recht zum Testament*).[82] He encourages the believer to stand defiantly on his right (*pochen und trotzig sein; darauf trotzen*).[83] This indicates that the strenuous effort to make consolation manageable by the believer's "asserting with certitude" God's favor toward him does not in fact produce spiritual consolation. Rather, it brings audacious defiance, which may sometimes bear a semblance to consolation but is nothing but a weird substitute for it, since it lacks the attitudes that are inseparable from true consolation, namely reverence, humility, and meekness.

However, we must also keep in mind that Luther was convinced that the faith he taught clung strictly to Christ and that it was faith in gifts bestowed by Christ.[84] He even emphasizes that we should "offer up" to God "ourselves and all that we have." Yet one must observe that Luther was here under a delusion (of which, though, he could have been cured had he attended to Cajetan's warning). Self-donation, after all, is the very opposite of the defiant assertion of one's claim and of one's turning his attention back to himself. A man who practices the one attitude cannot at the same time realize the other. Moreover, it is only among things which do "not necessarily and essentially belong to the Mass" that Luther mentions the "offering up" of "ourselves and all that we have in earnest prayer."[85]

During the Mass itself, Luther teaches, the Christian is to concentrate on himself: "You should above all attend to your own heart (*deines Herzens wahrnehmen*) so that you may believe Christ's words . . . in which he says to you and to all, 'This is my blood, a new testament, by which I bequeath to you forgiveness of sin and eternal life.' "[86] The same idea is brought out still more forcefully in Luther's *Large Catechism* (1529) where he teaches that a person at Mass should center his attention on the words *"for you,"* which are included in the words of consecration, and refer these words to himself. "He who accepts this and believes that it is true, he has it." "Therefore in your meditation slip yourself also into the *'you'* (*denke und bringe dich auch in das Euch*) ," namely into the phrase, "my blood shed for you."[87] The sermon of 1520 also emphasized the individualism of this practice by saying, "Each one takes and receives for himself alone as much as he believes and confides."[88]

Thus the spiritual practice to be performed at Mass is an exercise in reflexive faith, stimulated by the *"for you"* of the words of consecration and supported by the Real Presence of the "testator." *The Babylonian Captivity* says,

> "In actual fact, in the Mass there is nothing that we should pursue with greater diligence than — nay, this alone should be our concern — to gaze, meditate and ruminate upon these words, these promises of Christ which truly are the Mass itself, thus exercising, nourishing, increasing and strengthening our faith in those words . . . This is what he prescribes by saying, 'Do this in remembrance of me'."[89]

Thus even Our Lord's command to repeat the celebration of the Eucharist is twisted into an encouragement for reflexive faith. What matters in the Mass is the two words *"for you"* and the person's insistence on his "title to the testament" by realizing that he is one among those included in the "you."

Communion is not mentioned. In some later treatises, however, Luther does treat communion also, since, after all, the Lutheran celebration of the Lord's Supper, which began to develop from about 1523, is primarily a rite of communion. And other elements of eucharistic devotion, which had found no place in the revolutionary treatises of 1520, emerge in tracts and sermons of Luther's later career.[90]

Nevertheless, the leading ideas of the writings of 1520 remained the center of Luther's and later Lutheran doctrine and practice of the Lord's Supper. These ideas have virtually instituted a new rite, very different in its spiritual content from what Catholics in the East as well as in the West have at all times intended to do when celebrating the Eucharist. Only a remnant of continuity between the Catholic Eucharist and the Lord's Supper of Lutheranism is preserved, namely in the belief in the Real Presence.

The impact of reflexive faith is also clear from the role that Luther apportioned to thanksgiving in the Mass. From ancient times this sacrament has always been celebrated in a solemn rite of thanksgiving, with the result that at a very early time "thanksgiving" (*eucharistia*) became a name for the whole rite and the verb "to offer thanks" (*eucharistein*) once denoted what we today express by "to consecrate." In all liturgies the words of institution are embedded in a hymnic prayer praising God for his salvific deeds. Luther, on the contrary, held that praise and thanksgiving "do not necessarily and essentially belong to the Mass." He did admit that praise and thanksgiving "are more valuable, appropriate, powerful, and pleasant when performed in the gathering and community where people incite, move and animate each other, so that it powerfully rises up to God."[91] Here again reflexive faith has crippled cult. The performance of praise and thanksgiving in the Mass has become a matter of mere practical and psychological expediency. Taking all this into account, a modern Lutheran expositor of Luther's system has recognized that "the doctrine and celebration of the Lord's Supper has . . . doubtless become thinned down and impoverished in the Lutheran Church."[92] Unfortunately, the scholar failed to see the cause of this mutilation in Luther's reinterpretation based on the conception of reflexive faith.

5. Reflexive Faith and the Church

In 1518/19, Luther wrote a number of meditations which evidenced his deep understanding of the supernatural unity and fellowship that constitutes the essence of the Church. We presented above a specimen of this kind of thinking from his sermon on the Eucharist of 1519 (Section 4 of this chapter). The theme of our inquiry does not allow us to analyze more examples.[93] We confine ourselves to noting that such reflections form a remarkable complement to the more individualistic spirituality of Luther's earliest period and involve, when seen together with the documents from 1513 to 1517, the promise of a contribution to genuine reform of the Church.

By the end of 1520, however, the new doctrine of faith thoroughly permeated Luther's thought. It supplanted or maimed not only his theology of the cross but also a further development of his insights into the nature of the Church which had emerged in 1518/19. Interior freedom degenerated into principles that were distinctively subversive. In a number of Latin and German writings from the early twenties Luther consistently pursued his new course.[94] He proclaimed the principle of "evangelical liberty."[95] This liberty resides in man's conscience but also involves a license to abrogate in the Church everything that the believer judges to be mere "human ordinance."[96]

Yet Luther's intention was not solely to destroy. The doctrine of reflexive faith provided principles also for instituting a religious community. We cannot depict here the complex process which, controlled by the new conception of faith, led to the dissolution of the traditional constitution of the Church and its gradual replacement with a novel structure. We will confine ourselves to briefly pointing to three basic principles of the new community:

(a) the universal *sacerdotium* of all believers;

(b) word and sacrament as fundamental characteristics of the Church;

(c) the "exterior judgment" of the preachers as the guarantee of unity and orthodoxy.

All these principles emanate from the doctrine of reflexive faith. For, according to Luther, "the Church is born from the word of promise through faith, and by the same word she is nourished and preserved."[97]

(a) To do justice to Luther's doctrine of "priesthood of all believers" we must first make a distinction. In the New Testament *sacerdotium* and priesthood are not the same thing. In order to be able to express this distinction also when speaking of persons holding the sacerdotal office, we will here use the Latin *sacerdos* (Greek *hiereus,* Hebrew *kohen*). According to the New Testament, the only person holding the sacerdotal office in his own right is Jesus Christ. The ministry of the *kohen* in the Old Testament foreshadowed Christ's office. All members of the Body of Christ which is the Church participate in Christ's *sacerdotium* (1 Pet. 2, 5. 9; Apoc, 1, 6), though in different ways (1 Cor. 12, 29). The functions of bishop and priest are special modes of that participation, distinguished from that of the laity and founded in a sacramental qualification (Acts 14, 23; 1 Tim. 4, 14; 2 Tim. 1, 6). Early Christendom was keenly aware of the uniqueness of the position of bishops and priests, which bears but a remote analogy to that of a non-Christian *sacerdos.* This is reflected in the fact that the Greek words *presbyteros* and *episkopos* remained untranslated in Latin and even in the Germanic languages, though from about the third century onward *sacerdos* could be used to denote the bishop as the vicar of Christ. The English words *priest* and *bishop*; the German *Priester, Bischof*; and the Swedish *präst, biskop* are historical developments of those Greek words. Gradually, however, the notions of *priest* (and *bishop*) and *sacerdoes* coalesced, and the general *sacerdotium* of all baptized was on the point of being forgotten.

Now it is an undeniable merit of Luther's that he rediscovered the difference between *priest* and *sacerdos*.[98] He pointed out forcefully that the New Testament attributes the designation *sacerdos* only to Christ and, by participation, to the community of all baptized.[99] This would have been a real reinstatement of the principle of universal *sacerdotium* and an important contribution to reform, had Luther not at once spoilt his discovery by denying the essential difference between priesthood and laity. The medieval equation of *sacerdos* and priest, probably inevitable in the society of that time, had shifted the proportions but never changed the essence of the structure of the Church. But Luther's innovation, on the contrary, amounted to an overthrow of this structure. For according to his doctrine ecclesiastical ministers have no supernatural qualification distinguishing them from the laity. It is merely to maintain proper order that one from the community is elected or appointed to preach the Word and administer the sacraments.[100] Thus what Luther actually achieved was not a reinstatement of the universal *sacerdotium* but a general laicization.

Luther was right in maintaining that the *sacerdotium* of all Christians is grounded in Baptism.[101] But, as we have seen, Baptism was for him essentially a support of and an incentive for reflexive faith. Accordingly, what in his opinion qualifies every Christian for the priesthood or ministry is ultimately and essentially his faith. Everyone attending Mass is a priest through his faith; "faith is the proper priestly office."[102] Members of the nobility are qualified to take care of the reform of the Church insofar as they have the proper faith.[103] Conversely, Catholic priests are not real priests and it is doubtful whether in their Mass Christ's real Body and Blood is present, because they lack what Luther claims to be "proper Christian faith."[104]

(b) Since membership in the Church is constituted by the reflexive faith of its members, the objective basis of the Church is the same as that of faith: the word of promise and the sacraments. We have seen that these are the means to stir up, maintain, and strengthen reflexive faith. Accordingly, Luther teaches: "The sign by which you can externaly perceive where the Church is in the world, are baptism, the sacrament (of the altar), and the gospel."[105]

(c) In the first years after his breaking away from the Church Luther emphasized the individual's right and duty to judge all doctrines on the basis of his faith.[106] Later, however, when the Lutheran Church had begun to take form, he found it necessary to delegate, so to speak, part of the individual's certitude to the minister. The preacher must be certain of his vocation.[107] He must have the "exterior judgment" which enables him to judge doctrines for the benefit of his flock, to strengthen the faith of the weak, and to refute opponents.[108]

Once the role of reflexive faith is perceived, Luther's whole system manifests an impressive coherence. It is true that there were variations in the Protestant Luther's views on the nature of the Church, the ecclesiastical ministry, and the sacraments. There was surely a development from the revolutionary thrust of his beginnings to a more conservative position in his later years. Still, in his main principles, Luther remained remarkably consistent throughout his Protestant period. This consistency is usually interpreted as grounded in his doctrine of justification. The kind of faith, however, which alone, according to Luther, effects justification, is reflexive faith. Reflexive faith, correlated to the word of promise, determines the relative primacy of Holy Scripture. In relation to this word-bound faith all factors of the Christian life in turn receive their respective function. The law, charity, prayer, the sacraments, public worship, the ministry are all supposed ultimately to help stimulate, nourish, support and develop the all-important certitude which is equated with salvation.

CHAPTER VI

Disjointed Spirituality

1. Dread, Defiance and Pride

In this final chapter we will attempt to delineate the main features of the style of spiritual life that arose as a consequence of the doctrine and practice of reflexive faith. All the elements of this style have already been mentioned occasionally in foregoing chapters. Our present task is to complete the picture and to describe the interaction of some of the elements.

As we have already noted in the relevant contexts, Luther referred often to his own spiritual disturbances, for instance in the 1531-35 *Commentary on Galatians*. From the psychological viewpoint, these are certainly no different from the experiences of darkness he had in his early, pre-Protestant period. A comparison with St. Paul may perhaps help to elucidate the case. The zeal which the Pharisee Saul displayed in persecuting Christians was in its psychological background scarcely different from the active fervor he manifested after his conversion in the propagation and defense of the gospel. Spiritually, however, there is a gulf between the two attitudes. Similarly, if the anguish that Luther experienced in his early career is compared with the terrors of conscience which he describes in his later lectures, there will hardly emerge an essential difference on the psychological level. Yet there are striking differences, and these belong to the domain of spirituality. They are amenable to description. For a spirituality is not just a vague feeling but an attitude springing from a deliberate religious option. Accordingly, peculiarities and also derangements of spirituality can be expressed in theological propositions.

In his early period, Luther had willingly accepted the agony of desolation as a gracious visitation of God. His new doctrine of faith, however, implied that absence of the consoling certitude of God's favor was tantamount to the certitude of perdition. So he first sought to evade desolation, as his *Sermon on Penance* testifies (see Chapter V, Section 2). In the early parts of his second course of lectures on the Psalms, he strove desperately to argue away the legitimacy of that state of anguish (Chapter II, Section 2). Nevertheless, the troubles inevitably returned.

In the transition period of 1518/19 the remedies or prophylactics that Luther recommended against the terrors were prayer,[1] invocation of the name of the Lord,[2] and affective meditation on Christ's word. The latter Luther equated with spiritual bread eaten by and reinvigorating the believer.[3] It is significant that in the context of such recommendations there is no mention of the new concept of faith. While reflexive faith was making his troubles worse, Luther, fortunately, was for some time inconsistent enough to forget it in times of crisis. Perhaps at times the remedies actually proved successful. At any rate, the writings published in 1519 seem to reflect a spiritual atmosphere punctuated by the intermittent return of consolation and joy.

Then the victorious progress of the Reformation upheaval may for some years have appeared to give irrefutable confirmation to the truth of the new doctrine. Thus the certainty of victory may have functioned as a substitute for interior certitude. Characteristic is the Reformer's triumphant boasting in 1522: "Through us Christ is killing the Papacy . . . Soon people will say, *Expiravit* (It has drawn its last breath)."[4] But the interior problem was merely concealed by the external turbulence. Soon Luther experienced that the wind he had sown shot up as whirlwind. His principle that "in matters of faith every Christian is to himself

Pope and Church" engendered sectarian movements, and his encouragement of the overthrow of the established order of the Church was misused for political riots. Perhaps such experiences may have caused the unsolved interior problem to crop up again. The details of this development remain to be investigated. At any rate, in Luther's lectures in the second half of the 1520's, the problem emerges again, and it appears to have become less tractable through the intervening years.

Luther's early interior turmoils, described in 1519 as "storms of conscience,"[5] involved the temptation to despair of God's mercy.[6] This is a real temptation; for despair of God's mercy is a sin. But the common understanding of the word "temptation" in Christian parlance differs from the meaning it has in Luther's later spirituality, and this difference marks off a characteristic contrast between the spiritual disturbances of Luther's pre-Protestant period and the interior troubles of his later years. Although in his later works Luther can occasionally still speak of "temptations to despair,"[7] he generally uses the word "temptation" to denote the interior perturbations as such, the perturbations which the 1531-35 *Commentary on Galatians* describes as terror, dread, or struggles of conscience (*terrores, pavores, certamina, agones, luctae conscientiae*). One of the earliest occurrences of this usage is a passage, dating from early 1520, in Luther's second course of lectures on the Psalms. The description he gives here of the "spiritual tribulation" (*tribulatio spiritualis*[8]) is quite similar to that given in *resolutio* 15 (see above, Chapter II, Section 2). But there is a significant addition. The "tribulation" eventually turns out to be a "temptation." The person suffering it "ascribed it first to God having forgotten him and turned away from him . . . Then he ascribed it to the enemy (*inimicus*)." And this, Luther explains, is the right interpretation; for it is the Devil who, "though God ordains it thus, . . . is properly directing this temptation."[9]

But how is it that the Devil has taken over an operation once performed by God? A year earlier Luther had described it in the words: "When God begins to justify a man, he first condemns him, and he destroys him whom he wants to build up; he strikes him whom he wants to heal; he kills him whom he wants to quicken."[10] The change becomes intelligible when we consider a passage in Luther's second exposition of the *Our Father* (1519/20). This treatise speaks of the Evil One as "the cruel calumniator, accuser, and magnifier of our sin." The "trial of despair" is eventually specified as the "temptation of faith to despair."[11] The close association of disbelief and despair[12] reveals that the specific "temptation" Luther envisages here is loss of faith. Once faith is understood as necessarily including certitude of salvation, its loss, coinciding with the certitude of perdition, amounts to the most acute despair, and this, of course, must be a temptation from the Devil.

Reflexive faith thus brings about a total shift in a vital area of Christian spirituality. Luther's interior "tribulations" essentially consisted in pangs of conscience. According to Rom. 2, 15f the accusing verdict of man's conscience will be confirmed in the Last Judgment. Hence, Christian devotion has heard the call of the Holy Spirit in the voice of conscience, provided the conscience be not misled. Luther, on the contrary, traces this voice to the enemy of God. According to his lectures on Galatians in 1531, it is Satan who reminds man of the Law and of his sins![13] Thus the word "temptation" (*tentatio*) receives a novel sense, becoming virtually synonymous with "remorse." In Luther's German this innovation (which is very clear in his Latin) is somewhat disguised since he denotes the new type of temptation as *Anfechtung.* This expresses the idea that the Devil "challenges" or "attacks" the soul by reminding it of its sins. In English we sometimes render *Anfechtung* by "trial."

Luther's *Anfechtung* is specifically the danger of losing the certitude of salvation. Since it is impossible to retain this certitude permanently, Lutheran faith is inevitably accompanied by *Anfechtung*. This feature has been especially highlighted by recent existentialist Lutherans. On the one hand, they depict the salvation grasped certainly by faith as a watered down "future of existence." Beside this phantom the possibility of a certitude of perdition is scarcely envisaged. On the other hand, faith's experience of trial and temptation, its *Angefochtenheit,* has been raised by them to the level of a "constitutive element" in the very nature of faith.[14]

Luther, of course, knows how to substantiate his view from the Bible. He points to Apoc. 12, 10 where the Devil is called "the accuser."[15] He overlooks, however, that the Evil One accuses men "before our God," and not before their own conscience. In Luther's pre-Protestant period his use of Scripture was here more to the point. He cited 1 Jn. 3, 20 where it is said that it is man's heart, i.e. his conscience, that condemns him.[16]

If the Devil challenges or attacks the soul, how is one to counter him? While considering Luther's answer to this question, we will also have to ask about the methods he did *not* recommend or practice to get free of his disturbances. The contrast between what he did and what he did not (but ought to have done) will illuminate the derangement of his spirituality.

In the first place, it has to be noted that there is no prayer properly speaking. To be sure, in his terror Luther imagines that he perceives the imperceptible sighs of the Holy Spirit crying: "Abba, Father!" And he admonishes his hearers to cling to Christ's word of promise.[17] But, although the disturbances are essentially pangs of conscience, there is no trace of prayer of repentance. Instead, Luther at times directly addresses the Devil: "Holy Devil, thou wilt make me holy . . . Doest thou not hear that Christ was not handed over for saints or for righteousness but for sins? If I had no sin, I would have no need of Christ. Thou callest me a sinner; but this is precisely why I will be saved."[18]

This is interior defiance, the exact counterpart to the exterior defiance that Luther was offering to the Church.[19] No trace is left of the "sighing for grace" (*gemitus pro gratia*) that was characteristic of the spirituality of his pre-Protestant period. Instead, he simply presupposes Christ's grace to be at his disposal and he opposes it to the "Devil's" accusation by pointing to the word of promise and asserting his salvation through this word.

The absence of prayer shows once more the depersonalization and the anthropocentric turn of Luther's deranged spirituality. True prayer, which necessarily includes adoration, is a movement away from the ego; reflexive faith, on the contrary, being totally absorbed in anxiety for the own ego, cannot even think of prayer in its trials.

It need not be demonstrated at length that the solace which

Luther alleges to be attainable by the above-described procedure is not true spiritual consolation. Luther's German often enough says quite explicitly what it really is. For he frequently combines the words *Trost* (consolation, solace, comfort) and *Trotz* (obstinate defiance). For instance, he makes Christ say: "You shall set your consolation and defiance on me" (*Ihr sollt euren Trost und Trotz setzen auf mich*).[20] In Luther's mind the meanings of the two words seem to overlap. The corresponding verbs, trotzen (to defy) and *sich getrösten* (to find consolation, to be confident), are almost synonyms in his language. For example, in the following sentence one would expect an expression like "to be confident" or "to find consolation," but instead Luther uses *trotzen* and even intensifies the meaning by adding a second, stronger word: "A person should freely and defiantly boast of (*trotzen*) and presume on (*sich vermessen*) all things of Christ being his own without his doing works, out of pure grace."[21]

The structure of Luther's Protestant spirituality is certainly the prototype of modern "dialectical" thinking. But his dialectic is anything but an interesting intellectual play. He posits the necessity of one's asserting with certitude his own state of grace. He persistently ignores (though he knows it, as his exposition of the *Our Father* of 1517/19 testifies) that such a position cannot be held. Incertitude proves unavoidable. The very practice of reflexive faith makes it develop into the despair, which is a degenerate form of his previous darkness. Since this darkness once terminated in — or several times alternated with — consolation, Luther thinks he can deliberately change despair into consolation by applying the proper method. The method is the practice of assertive faith. But the result can only be a disfigured form of and a poor substitute for consolation, i.e. interior defiance and obstinacy, *Trotz* desperately equated with *Trost*.

As he had done with his earlier style of interior life, so Luther turned his system of deranged spirituality also into a general norm. In his lectures on Isaiah (1527) he has briefly described the procedure that is to make a man a Christian: "First to terrify, to detect one's sins, to bring one to know what he himself is, to humiliate the heart; then, if one is driven to despair, the other function [of Scripture] follows, namely cheering one up (*erectio*), consoling the conscience, [by] the promises."[22] If this method has been successful and a person later feels himself again threatened by the Law or the prospect of the Last Judgment, he must recall words of promise and assert his state of grace. This asserting can and must be done with "pride."

"Holy pride" is a term used by the editor of the 1535 *Commentary on Galatians*. It denotes another aspect of the same attitude that Luther elsewhere describes as "obstinate defiance" (*Trotz*). As early as 1520 he taught that one claiming his "title to the testament" (*jus testamenti*) should go to receive the Blessed Sacrament "with proud confidence" (*superba fiducia*).[23] Like the false consolation of defiance, this pride also rests on a remaining substratum of despair. The editor of the Galatians' commentary even says, surely in accordance with Luther's mind, "The conscience deems it a great presumption and pride to arrogate to itself this glory," namely, to be in God's grace.[24] Nevertheless, Luther thought that to secure salvation one must put down scruples and maintain "holy pride."[25] This pride consists in a man's being certain of being loved by God; it coexists or alternates with a "humility" caused by man's consciousness of being a sinner deserving of God's wrath.

In this form a remnant of the idea of humility, which was one of the chief constituents of Luther's pre-Protestant spirituality, survives in the system of reflexive faith. Humility has become identical with that dread which is the presupposition of a person's assertion of his being in God's grace.[26] The difference between the two spiritualities becomes clearest when one considers that in Luther's early period faith and trust were closely associated with humility,[27] whereas in his deranged spirituality faith has become proud and defiant.

2. Escapism

The defiant claiming of one's "title to the testament" is a pure makeshift. It rests on the enduring basis of threatening despair. When Gerhard Ebeling says: "It belongs to the very essence of faith to be threatened, to be called in question, to be tempted (*Angefochtenheit*)," [28] he is describing exactly the system of Luther's reflexive faith and he is missing the nature of real Christian faith. In both Luther's and Ebeling's case presence of temptation is plainly the consequence of the self-contradictory adventure of an anthropocentric faith. But we know now that the implications in Luther's concept are very closely connected with his own life and experience. Therefore, the basis of faith's essential experience of temptation in Ebeling's thought appears to be very different from Luther's spirituality. Nevertheless, there is an intrinsic connection. Luther's "temptations" were the outcome of the deadly stress produced by the first effort of a man-oriented trend to assert itself within the uncontested framework of a decidedly theocentric and christocentric religion. Since Luther's time the same trend has forced faith to withdraw to the position of a "religionless Christianity." Anthropocentrism has reached its last stage before coinciding with professed atheism. This situation causes a new kind of interior convulsion, and this is the contemporary form of faith's essential experience of temptation. The whole nightmare of "tempted faith" vanishes once the reflexivity of faith is renounced. But for many it seems arduous to get rid of an inveterate evil . . .

The positive background of Luther's dread and "temptations" was his exceedingly keen awareness of the majesty of God. This awareness was no less vivid in his pre-Protestant period than it was later. In a sermon he gave on August 15, 1517 (i.e., a few months before he conceived of his new doctrine of faith), Luther quotes Proverbs 25, 27 which in the incorrect Vulgate text is as follows: "He who scrutinizes the majesty, will be oppressed by the glory (*Qui scrutator est majestatis, opprimetur a gloria*)." Luther warns against searching into God's majesty because this will lead either to pride or to terror.[29] Terror of God (*pavor Dei*) in its turn was given a positive value in a passage, dating approximately from early 1516, of his *Lectures on Romans*: it is an incentive to humility and even a sign of being elected by God.[30] The proper road for ascending to the knowledge of God, according to the sermon of 1517, is the humanity of Christ: this is "Jacob's ladder." God has out of his mercy adapted himself to our weakness in the Incarnation so that we, contemplating his life and suffering, may be stirred to love and imitate him, to fulfill the

Law out of love for him, and finally to become capable of knowing, without fear, God's "power and wisdom."[31]

Fourteen years later, in Luther's lectures on Galatians, the caution against speculation and the simile of Jacob's ladder recur. The context illuminates the way reflexive faith has in the meantime transformed Luther's spirituality. The published commentary of 1535 deviates here from the lecture notes because the editor has omitted or qualified some of Luther's shocking statements. In the following two paragraphs we will work from the lecture notes.

Dread of God has reached a point where Luther virtually renounces the doctrine of the Trinity. He alleges that not only Jews and Muslims but also Papists and Protestant sectarians remove Christ the Mediator (*auferunt ex oculis, amoliuntur de medio*) and worship God the Father. Christian theology, on the contrary, "excludes" this God (*nos excludimus eum*). The reason for this exclusion is this: "When the question is how to behave with God and toward God, drop all speculation on the Majesty. And when you have to stand up to sin and death, let go of God (*lass Gott fahren*), for he is intolerable here."[32]

Luther does not, however, intend to "exclude" God the Father from dogma (nor even from the liturgy). Doctrinal disputes, he teaches, are "another field," where dogma must be defended. Yet,

"when the issue is righteousness and grace, when death, sin and the Law are at stake, things that a Christian is concerned about, then we must see that we know of no God, but rather seize (apprehend) the God Incarnate and the Human God. . . . In matters . . . of our salvation one has simply to abstain from all ponderings and speculations on the Majesty and simply to cling to the man Christ who offers himself as the Mediator. . . . One should ascend by Jacob's ladder . . . Take refuge at the manger (*rapias te in praesepe*) and the Mother's lap and look at [Jesus] lying at the mother's breast, growing up, and dying; then you can *escape from all terrors*. . . . Another point, the confirmation of our faith, is that Christ is true God. . . . The Father bestows remission of sins and peace. Christ gives the same things. Now to give grace and remission of sins . . . is not the work of a creature but of the one Majesty alone. . . . Christ is capable to give and create these things; therefore he must be true God."[33]

These teachings imply that Luther sets up a sharp antithesis between *God in himself* and *God for us*. God in himself — God the Father and, by implication, the Trinity — certainly remains an uncontested object of faith. But when the contents of faith are at stake wherein man himself is vitally concerned then God turns into an object of dread and terror. For Luther the idea of God's Majesty is inseparably tied up with the idea of the Judge. Hence God's Majesty reminds him of his sins as well as of the insufficiency of his good works, and causes him to tremble. It becomes understandable here, and is borne out also by general psychological observation, that at the bottom of Luther's substitute consolation of interior defiance there must have been a dread and despair which he never managed to cope with. This dread prevented him from ever developing a trinitarian devotion. On the contrary, *escape* from God's terrifying Majesty, i.e. from God the Father and the Trinity, forms an essential part of his piety. It is noteworthy in this connection that in the liturgy of his "German Mass" he omitted the *Gloria in excelsis*. The reason may have been the words, "We give you thanks for your great glory." How could Luther have invited a community to thank God for the glory which terrified him and from which he sought to escape?

Though Luther can leave his own self out of consideration while he debates questions theoretically, he can never do so in his piety where he stands face to face with God. Reflexive faith has accustomed him to constantly turn his attention back on his own self and even to regard this practice as decisive for his own salvation. Consequently, the power to love God has been crippled. Trinitarian devotion, however, is impossible unless it be an act of self-forgetting love. As St. Irenaeus says, God grants himself to be known by those who *love* him.[34]

Both in thinking of God the Father and in thinking of Christ Luther cannot forget himself. But while he feels terrified in confronting the Father, the vision of God Incarnate comforts him. For Christ is the author of the word of promise. In his lowly humanity there is nothing frightening — and yet this humble man is God, and not only God, but the God who forgives sin. So it is only in realizing the divinity of Christ that Luther can, without being terrified, think of God while continuing to look back at himself. For here the self enters into the mental vision in the form of the awareness, "I am saved." Christ is "God for us," nay, "God for *me.*"

Luther's escapist devotion involves a sharp severance of dogma from spirituality and a fateful break within the trinitarian as well as the christological dogmas. While continuing to profess both dogmas wholeheartedly, he directs his followers to disregard vital parts of them precisely in the practice of devotion. The believer, while not being allowed to forget his own self, is to forget the Trinity precisely in the most crucial moments of his religious life. One must ask whether under such circumstances the dogma can in the long run retain its position in the framework of religion. In Christology the situation is similar. Christ's humanity is the "Jacob's ladder," but not in the sense that it leads our contemplation up to adore the Triune God and to respond to God's call. The ascent by the ladder stops at a point where the devotee, while realizing the divinity of Christ, need not lose sight of his own self. In true Catholic spirituality the dogma presents guidance to religious life. Both are thus a unity. Luther's disjointed spirituality has broken apart this unity. The cause of the break has been the obligation to reflect on the ego within the very encounter with God: "So you must here above all attend to your heart." (*Also musst du hier vor allen Dingen deines Herzens wahrnehmen.*) [35]

Thus the shift to anthropocentrism not only caused a perpetual crisis in Luther's spiritual life, to be described by words like lack of love for God, dread, despair, defiance, false consolation, and escapism, but has also gained a significance quite independent of the interior life of this one man who initiated the shift. In a larger perspective, this shift foretells a breakdown of dogma and eventually of faith in the other-worldly reality of God. Is it too bold to see at the end of this escapist movement an ideology which renounces God as dead and replaces supernatural salvation by an inner-worldly ideal which somehow still manages to acknowledge Jesus?

3. Antithetical Correlationism

In Luther's theology and spirituality the reflexivity of faith appears intimately intertwined with a thought pattern which we will denote as antithetical correlationism or, briefly, antitheticalism. It consists in the positing of spiritual opposites as correlative in such a way that the one does not exist without the other. Thus Luther correlates, for example, sin with grace, despair with assurance, God's wrath with His love. One member strictly presupposes the other. Sometimes he sets up correlative antitheses where Catholic doctrine finds harmony, for instance between law and gospel, between faith and love. We will treat here chiefly the antithesis between sin and grace.

Like Luther's penchant for reflection, his antitheticalism lives on vigorously in our own time. The prominent Lutheran existentialist Gerhard Ebeling, in his widely-read introduction to Luther's thought, has made Luther's antitheticalism an interpretative principle for the Reformer's thought,[36] and in his book on Christian faith[37] he has given a modernized description of faith which can be analyzed as reflexive to the point of being man-centered. The modish thought pattern of "dialectics" is ultimately and essentially an extension of Luther's antitheticalism. It is ultimately the impact of Luther's doctrine of reflection that has in modern usage narrowed the meaning of the word "existential" to denote what decisively concerns the existence of a *human individual* in a crucial *individual situation*.

Correlative antitheses were a constituent of Luther's style of thinking even in his early career. An example is the antithesis of God's judgment and justice to which we referred at the beginning of Chapter II. However, in spite of formal similarities, it appears that the general meaning of antitheses in Luther's early period was different from the one they have in his later thought. With some simplification, one may say that in Luther's pre-Protestant period an antithesis marks an opposition only for a first approximation, only at a superficial level. It is a challenge to plumb the depth of the divine economy. Thus in reality there is no contrast between God's judgment and justice. Similarly, when Luther says in his *Lectures on Romans* that "he who wants to be just must become a sinner,"[38] he is intending to forcibly exhort the sinner to recognize and confess what he really *is,* because no one can expect grace who is not willing to confess his sin. Most probably, antitheses of the latter kind also reflect Luther's spirituality of darkness which was characterized by an uneasy suspense between the consciousness of sin and consolation.

With the emergence of Luther's new doctrine of faith, however, antitheses receive a new function in his thought. We have seen that Luther intensified assertion to obstinate defiance, in order to cope with his spiritual "tribulations." Now, as we shall presently see more in detail, insistence on antitheses is a procedure perfectly suited to the practice of interior defiance. This use of the pattern of antithetical thinking involves a shift in the meaning of the positing of antitheses. The contrast is no more a mere semblance. The negative part of the contrast receives a positive function. The antithesis of two contrasting positions becomes a sort of ontological structure.

Antitheses of this kind occur in Luther's works from 1519 onward. In his second course of lectures on the Psalms the idea occurs that it is "most dangerous" for a man

> to be left in many merits and graces of God until his death. Then he will never learn to place his hope in God. Therefore it happens through God's mercy that men fall not only into perturbations of conscience but sometimes also, if they are of a coarser and harder nature, into downright sin, like fornication and similar crimes, and God is constrained to preserve them with such care as to lead them against his mercy to his mercy and to free them through sin from sin.[39]

Here not only the perturbation of conscience, which includes man's *acknowledging* himself to be a sinner, but man's *being* a sinner is posited as a prerequisite for being saved. Sometimes even a man must lose grace in order to learn to hope and thus be saved. Sin thus becomes a prerequisite for salvation, more important than grace! We can only observe that grace has been ontologically tied to its opposite, sin.

> At another place, Luther says in the same course of lectures, He who wants to become righteous must needs become a sinner; he who wants to become . . . a Catholic Christian, let him become . . . a heretic, and infidel. . . . As Paul said, 'If any one among you thinks he is wise in this age, let him be-

come a fool that he may become wise' (1 Cor. 3, 18) . . .
(God) has ordained to make (men) . . . righteous through sin,
. . . Catholics through heresy, Christians through unbelief . . .
You cannot become in God what you want to be unless you
first become in yourself and among men what he wants you to
be. Now he wants that you become in yourself and among men
what you really are, that is to say, a sinner . . .[40]

It may seem risky to draw conclusions from this passage which
betrays extreme excitement, and more risky still if we consider
the passage in its wider context. However, if we compare it
with the preceding quotation, with Luther's quotation from St.
Paul, and with other statements of Luther's later years, then
a content emerges which is independent of a temporary emo-
tion. St. Paul does not say that God makes men righteous *through*
sin, but this is precisely the idea suggested in the quotation we
gave in the preceding paragraph. Moreover, the mention of heresy
is illustrative. If a man becomes a heretic in the view of other
people then these may be mistaken. But if he becomes a heretic
in his own eyes then there are two possibilities: either he acknowledges that he is a heretic and by this same acknowledgment
he ceases to be such; or he knows that he is a heretic and yet
decides to remain such, and then he is really a heretic. It may
be significant that Luther's wording does not exclude this latter
possibility.

But, however we may interpret the last-quoted passage, in
Luther's later writings antithetical correlationism occurs in a still
more developed form. For now assertive faith establishes a type
of synthesis by bridging over the chasm of the antithesis of sin
and grace. Yet it never removes or neutralizes the antagonism.
It is only the assertion that the antithesis as such has a positive
meaning.

The following sentence from 1520 brings out vividly the idea
of synthesis: "A Christian or one baptized . . . can never, even
though he want to, forfeit his salvation even through ever so many
sins, unless he decides not to believe."[41] The faith meant here is
the belief "that we are saved" (*nos esse salvos*).[42] It bridges over
the chasm between sinful man and God's grace regardless of
whether one perseveres in sin.

The idea that sin is a prerequisite for faith's positing of grace in opposition to it is most forcefully brought out in Luther's addresses to the Devil. The 1535 publication on Galatians, at this place faithfully working up into sentences the somewhat incoherent lecture notes, makes the believer say to Satan, "If you call me a sinner you do not terrify me but you console me exceedingly."[43] The underlying idea is that Christ has suffered for sinners, and hence I must be a sinner in order to obtain the grace of forgiveness, and this grace is given to me the moment I assert that I have it.

This is the context in which we have to read Luther's famous dictum, *"Pecca fortiter."* This occurs in a letter he wrote to Melanchthon on August 1, 1521:

> "God does not save fictitious sinners. Be a sinner and sin bravely (*pecca fortiter*); but trust still more bravely and rejoice in Christ who is the victor over sin, death and world. We must sin so long as we are here. . . . It is sufficient that we, through the wealth of God's glory, should have acknowledged the Lamb who takes away the sin of the world. Sin will not tear us from him even though we fornicate and kill thousands of times in one day."[44]

Both ideas are brought out here with unchecked obtrusiveness: first, sin is the prerequisite for grace to be obtained by faith; second, precisely the synthesis that faith establishes between sin and grace necessitates the persistence of sin.

Similar ideas recur nine years later in a letter which Luther wrote to a friend who (like others) had been infected with Luther's interior troubles. Luther advises his friend to address Satan thus:

> "I avow indeed that I am guilty of death and hell; but what can come of that, after all? Wilt thou therefore condemn me for eternity? By no means, for I know one who has suffered and satisfied for me, whose name is Jesus Christ, the Son of God."[45]

The last quotation is an example also of Luther's practice of interior defiance. In fact, his antithetical positing of sin and grace in correlation, though implying a sort of ontological structure, is primarily meant as a practice of defiant self-assertion against the danger of despair. From this perspective, the antithesis, bridged over by the apparent synthesis of assertive faith, turns out to be a virtual affirmation of what St. Paul indignantly rejects in saying: "Are we to continue in sin that grace may abound? By no means!" (Rom. 6, 1f).

In previous chapters we have already noted the antitheses of gospel and law, of love and faith, of Christ the example and Christ the gift. In all these cases it is reflexive, assertive faith that establishes a sort of synthesis.

Of special interest is the antithesis between God's wrath and God's love because both poles are here posited in God whereas the apparent synthesis is located in man. Luther could say: "As you think [God to be] so he becomes. If you believe that he is angry then he is so."[46] "For to each one God is such as he is believed to be."[47] Here we meet again the trends we already noted in other contexts: first, toward making God's behavior manageable by man's thinking of it, second, toward the inceptive stage of an idealism that posits existence as dependent on consciousness. To be sure, Luther did not conceive these trends abstractly. But it cannot be denied that they actually exist in his system. Thus there is more than one movement in the later history of modern thought which is indebted to suggestions that can be traced to Martin Luther.

NOTE: With the exception of Luther's exposition of the Creed in the *Small Catechism* (Chapter I, Section 1), all texts quoted have been translated by the author from their original languages. Scripture is ordinarily quoted according to the Revised Standard Version. Footnote references to texts from Luther are to the "Weimar Edition" of his works, *D. Martin Luthers Werke, Kritische Gesamtausgabe* (Weimar, 1883ff). The references give the volume number, page number, and in most cases the line on which the relevant passage begins. The abbreviation "WA" refers to this source, when it would not otherwise be clear. "WBr" refers to Luther's letters, "WDtB" to his German Bible, and "WT" to his Tabletalk — according to the three further divisions of the Weimar Edition.

Notes

NOTES TO CHAPTER I

1. *The Book of Concord — The Symbols of the Evangelical Lutheran Church* (St. Louis, 1957), pp. 160f. Translation by F. Bente and W. H. T. Dau.
2. 7,218,16. The Calvinistic *Heidelberg Catechism,* Question 52, presents the same teaching.
3. 30I,187,9.
4. 26,509,14.
5. An allusion to Jas. 2, 19.
6. 2,458,20.
7. 2,491,30.
8. 2,249,5.
9. 39I,45. Thesis 24.
10. Thesis 25.
11. 39I,45. Thesis 12.
12. PG 44,893. *Gregorii Nysseni Opera,* ed. Jaeger, Vol. 6 (Leiden, 1960), 183, line 8ff.
13. F. Gogarten, *Luthers Theologie* (Tübingen, 1967), 77. WA 26, 65,20.
14. St. Ambrose, *Tractatus in Ev. sec. Lucam,* II, 41 (*Sources Chrétiennes,* Vol. 45 [Paris, 1956], 91).
15. Gabriel Tissot, *ibid.,* 27.
16. Gogarten, *Luthers Theologie,* 75. WA 10I,1,71,6.
17. 32,266,14.
18. 3,68,33.
19. 1,75,8.
20. 1,121,10.
21. See Hans Urs von Balthasar, *Spiritus Creator* (Einsiedeln, 1967), 76-91.
22. 7,215,1.
23. *Summa theologiae,* II-II, 2, 2.
24. *Tractatus in Johannis Ev.,* 29, 6. *Sermo* 144, 2.
25. For example 2,458,22; 38,198, 15; 39II,264,11; 40I,285,23; 57 III,169,12.
26. 40I,545,7.26.
27. Louis Bouyer, *Reformatorisches Christentum und die eine Kirche* (Würzburg, 1959), 149. The French original of this book, *Du protestantisme à l'église,* was published in 1954.
28. 8,323,13.
29. For example in *Kerygma und Mythos,* Vol. 2, ed. H. W.

Bartsch (Hamburg-Volksdorf, 1952), 201.

30. Gerhard Ebeling, *Das Wesen des christlichen Glaubens* (Siebenstern edition, Munich & Hamburg, 1965), 173.
31. WT 5, 242. Nr. 5562.
32. 2,46,16.
33. 5,395,12.
34. 6,206,12.
35. 18,769,16.
36. 40II,343,1.
37. 17I,203,29.
38. 18,769,18.
39. 7,25,9.
40. 42,48,18.
41. *Wesen des christlichen Glaubens*, 154.
42. 30I,133,1.
43. 40I,576f.
44. 12,188,12.16.
45. 18,653,14.
46. 6,215,18.
47. 25,332,5. Cf. 31II,434,34.
48. 25,331,7.
49. 25,330,38. Cf. 31II,434,7.
50. 40I,578f.
51. 10I,1,337,17.
52. 12,422,32; WDtB 7,10,6.
53. 39I,44,1.

54. 40I,578,22.
55. 39I,83,26.
56. WA 6, pp. 204-216.
57. WDtB 7,9,30. Cf. 10III, pp. 335ff.
58. *Die Theologie Martin Luthers* (Gütersloh, 1962), 56-58.
59. *Luther — Einführung in sein Denken* (Tübingen, 1 9 6 4), 196f.
60. *Luthers Theologie*, 76, 86f.
61. *De Trinitate* IV, c. 3.
62. See E. Iserloh, "Sacramentum et exemplum," in *Reformata Reformanda* (Jedin Festschrift) (Münster, 1965), Vol. I, 247-264.
63. The old combination of *sacramentum et exemplum* turned up again in a disputation held in 1538. WA 39I,350; Thesis 25. In another disputation *donum* and *sacramentum* are identified. 39I,462,21.
64. 10I,1, pp. 11-12; 15,778,2.
65. 40II, pp. 41-43.
66. 40I,448,6.
67. 40I,233,8.
68. 40I, p.285f.

NOTES TO CHAPTER II

1. 57III,79,20; 1,354,27.
2. A key passage is Luther's exposition of Ps. 71:2, WA 3, pp.462ff. For a clearer version of this confused text, see *Luthers Werke in Auswahl,* Vol. 5, ed. E.Vogelsang (2nd ed., Berlin 1955), pp. 151ff.
3. WA 3,463,17. Vogelsang's edition, p. 155, line 33.
4. WA 3,646,20.
5. "Non autem mortificamur nisi per fidem, quae humiliat sensum proprium et subjicit alterius." 56,416,8. [Fides] qua homo sensum suum captivat in verbum crucis." 56,419,16.
6. 1,123,33.
7. 1,118,37. For a comprehensive presentation of the spirituality taught by Luther in his pre-Protestant period see Jared Wicks, *Man Yearning for Grace* (Washington, 1968).
8. 56,204,14.
9. 56,79,15; 56,pp.369f.

10. Wicks, *op.cit.*, Chapter IV, note 84.
11. 57III,114,13.
12. 57III,169,10.
13. PL 183,383.
14. 56,pp.369f.
15. 57III,170,5-171,4.
16. 57III,191,24.
17. 56,pp.391ff.
18. 1,557,33.
19. 56,424,27; 57III,188,10.
20. 54,186,8.
21. 1,189,37.
22. 2,117,10.
23. 2,115,13.
24. 2,116,36.
25. 5,159,2.
26. 5,173,2.
27. 5,171,4ff.
28. 2,49,10ff.
29. 2,113,15-114,4.
30. 2,458,20.
31. 5,124,20-40.
32. For example in the German "sermons" *On Meditating on the Holy Passion of Christ, On How to Prepare Oneself for Death,* and on the sacraments of Penance, Baptism, and the Eucharist (all in WA 2).
33. 7, pp.222ff.
34. Thomas Merton, *New Seeds of Contemplation* (London, 1962), 165.
35. A presentation of the history of the divisive Reformation was recently given by Erwin Iserloh in: *Handbuch der Kirchengeschichte,* ed. H.Jedin, vol.4: Reformation, Katholische Reform und Gegenreformation (Freiburg, 1967).
36. See Gerhard Hennig, *Cajetan*

und Luther (Stuttgart, 1966), p.56,n.44.
37. Hennig, *op.cit.,* 78.
38. Hennig, *op.cit.,* 49.
39. WBr 1,no.110,p.238,lines 73-76.
40. Hennig, *op.cit.,* 56.
41. 2,13,6-10.
42. Denzinger, *Enchiridion Symbolorum,* no.824.
43. 56, pp. 218, 447, 450.
44. 56, pp. 249 and 251.
45. WBr 1, no. 126, pp. 284ff.
46. 2,17,37; 2,18,3.
47. 5,227,33.
48. 2,605,12-29.
49. 40I,181,6.21; 40I, 642,31; 40II, 47,26.
50. WBr 1, no.100,p.217,60-63; no. 110, p.238,71.76.81; no. 178, p. 402,38; WA 2,17,19; 2,39,29.
51. WBr 1,no.121,p.270,12.
52. A key passage: WA 5,pp.339ff.
53. See, e.g., 8,pp.315.613.683f.
54. 10II,107,3. On February 9, 1521, Luther wrote to his superior Johannes Staupitz: "Tibi adest nimia humilitas, sicut mihi nimia superbia" (WBr 2, no.376;p.263,27). On March 5, 1522, he wrote to the Prince Elector Friedrich: "However, I now see that my excess of humility will result in a disadvantage of the gospel and the Devil will occupy the whole place if I leave him only a hand's breadth. Therefore my conscience forces me to take another course" (WBr 2,no.455;p.455,46).
55. 10II,107,11.
56. 5,407,35.

NOTES TO CHAPTER III

33. Cf. Heinrich Schlier, *Der Brief an die Galater,* 12th ed. (Göttingen, 1962), pp.96f with footnote 4 and p.103, footnote 1.
34. Cf. Hans Urs von Balthasar, *Sponsa Verbi* (Einsiedeln. 1961), 174ff.
35. v.Balthasar, *op.cit.,* 177.
36. 40I, pp.91ff. Cf. 2,458,20.
37. 25,pp.330f. Cf. 31II,p.434.
38. 6,529,32.
39. Althaus, *op.cit.,* 375f.
40. Cf. Chapter IV, Section 1.
41. Althaus, *op.cit.,* 384.
42. 36,462,4.
43. 2,458,22; 38,198,15; 39II,264, 11; 40I,285,23; 57III,169,12.
1. 40II,51,1.15; 52,4.22. Cf. Althaus, *Die Theologie Martin Luthers,* pp.55f, footnotes 27 and 28.
2. Althaus, *op.cit.,* p.55.
3. Althaus, *op.cit.,* p.40.
4. 10I,1,130,14.
5. 10II,90,10.
6. 10I,1,129,9; 130,1.
7. G.Ebeling, *Das Wesen des christlichen Glaubens,* pp.80-82, and 175.
8. 56,338,14; 57II,59,18.
9. 36,10,2-5.
10. G.Ebeling, *Luther,* 127.
11. *Ibid.,* 134.
12. Althaus, *op.cit.,* 231.

13. Althaus, *loc.cit.*
14. 40II,43,7.
15. For example, 18,pp.680-695.
16. 8,323,18; 39II,264,13; 40I,426, 2.17. Althaus, *op.cit.,* 48 and 223.
17. 10III,423,17; 40III,50,3. Althaus, *op.cit.,* 48f., footnotes 3 and 4.
18. 2,13,12-16,3.
19. 2,13,29.
20. 2,13,23.
21. 2,13,33.
22. 2,14,16.
23. 2,15,2.
24. 2,14,2.23.
25. 2,14,5.
26. For the association of *Trotz* (defiant obstinacy) and *Trost* (consolation) in the Protestant Luther's thought, see below Chapter VI, Section 1.
27. See Chapter II, Section 1 and J. Wicks, *Man Yearning for Grace,* Chapter III, Section 5; and Chapter IV, Section 12; and Chapter IV, note 88.
28. 40II,6,20.
29. *Das Wesen des christlichen Glaubens,* 173.
30. WBr 1,no.110,p.234,48.
31. 6,528,34; 8,594.
32. 40I,299,29.

NOTES TO CHAPTER IV

1. 1,321,18.24.
2. *Apologia Confessionis Augustanae,* Art.III (De dilectione et impletione legis),no.7; Art.V (De poenitentia), no. 34.
3. 11,185,5.

4. 56,248,8.
5. 57II,97,28.
6. 56,249,8.
7. 2,552,10; 560,13; 562,9.33; 575, 3.
8. 2,591,26.

9. 40II,3,22.26.
10. Cf. H.Schlier, *Der Brief an die Galater,* 12th ed. (Göttingen, 1962), 176-188.
11. 2,499,26; 560,22.
12. 31II,69,27; 25,122,19.
13. 40I,274,22.
14. 40I,558,6.24.
15. 40I,pp.266-281.
16. 40I,275,12.
17. Thomas Aquinas, *Summa theologiae* II-II,4,3: "Caritas dicitur forma fidei, inquantum per caritatem actus fidei perficitur et formatur." The Council of Trent has not dogmatized the term "informed with love" but has rejected Luther's doctrine that love has no share in man's justification. See Denzinger, no. 821.
18. 2,536,35.
19. 40I,pp.571-593.
20. 6,204,25; 209,33.
21. See above, Chapter III, Section 3, and Althaus, *op.cit.,* 375.
22. 39II,248,11. Cf. 40I,577,12.29.
23. 10III,225,35.
24. Althaus, *op.cit.,* 357 and 372.
25. WDtB 7,11,10.
26. 7,36,3.
27. 40I,234,25.
28. 40II,61,15.
29. 40II,61,17.
30. 40I,181,11. The lecture notes read as follows (40I,180,10): "sed hoc quaerimus, ut simus nos salvi et ipsi, ut gloria Dei stet et justitia fidei erhalten. Si hoc, Sanctissimum dicerem Papam, non solum osculari pedes, sed portare in manibus. Si impetrare possumus, quod Deus solus justificet per gratiam." The 1538 edition differs from that of 1535 in that it replaces "Hoc impetrato" with "Si igitur Papa nobis concesserit." The latter reading seems more in place because *impetrare* involves asking and it is not known that Luther asked the Pope to do what would have amounted to confirming once more the decrees of the Second Synod of Orange.
31. Denzinger, no.811.
32. Denzinger, nos.178 and 180.
33. Denzinger, nos.800 and 821.
34. Heiko Oberman, *The Harvest of Medieval Theology* (Grand Rapids, 1967), 153 and 155.
35. 1,224,28; 225,3.
36. 40I,pp.164ff; 225,23; pp.239ff; pp.436ff; p.606; 40II,pp.34-39; pp.79ff; 39II,pp.191-193.
37. For example 25,331,27; 31II, 434,20.
38. 39II,p.238. Theses 8,12, and 16f.
39. 40I,444,12.
40. 39II,192,3.
41. For example, on the nine pages 40I, 228-236, *apprehendere* occurs fifteen times in the commentary.
42. 18,pp.186-188 and pp.693-695.
43. Augustine, Letter 194,5,19; *Sermo* 131,8; *Tractatus in Joh. Ev.* 3,10; *De trinitate* 3,10. Council of Trent: Denzinger, no.810.
44. 18,695,14.
45. 36,pp.352ff.
46. Cited WA 36, *xxviii.*
47. 36,pp.358-360.
48. 36,372,3.
49. 36,363,18.
50. 36,374,4.
51. 36,373,13.
52. 25,331,7.
53. 36,365,8.
54. 7,p.26f

55. 40I,241,16.
56. 40I,212,11.
57. 17II,53,5.
58. 39I,23,7.
59. 40I,642,31; 40II,47,26. Cf. 40II, 51,8 and 52,13.
60. 40I,241,21.
61. 40I,234,18.
62. 40I,577,28. Althaus, *op.cit.*, 215 and 375.
63. 40I,427,11.
64. G.Ebeling, *Luther*, 185.
65. 40II,38,1.
66. 40II,37,26.
67. 25,95,15.
68. For example 40II,36,3.
69. 40II,62,4.
70. 40II,62,13. Cf. 40II,83,19.
71. 40II,49,4.
72. 40II,49,25.
73. 31II,14,21.
74. 40II,79,10.26; 80,8.25.
75. F.Gogarten, *Verhängnis und Hoffnung der Neuzeit* (Stuttgart, 1953), 202.
76. F.Gogarten, *Was ist Christentum?* (Göttingen, 1956), 85.
77. *Ibid.*,31.

NOTES TO CHAPTER V

1. The most important among these is the *Treatise on Indulgences*. See Jared Wicks' analysis in *Theological Studies* 28 (1967), 481-518.
2. 1,539,36.
3. *Summa theologiae* III,84,3 ad 3.
4. See Heiko Oberman, *The Harvest of Medieval Theology* (Grand Rapids, 1967), pp.147f, 156, and 159.
5. *Sententiae* IV,18,8.
6. Quotations translated in the following are from WA 1, pp. 539-543.
7. 1,pp.593-596.
8. 1,558,5.
9. *Pax* and *fides* virtually identified: 1,542,7. *Pax, remissio* and *certitudo* virtually identified: 1, 542,14-17.
10. 1,324,28.
11. 1,320,33.
12. 1,320,42.
13. 1,321,15.
14. 1,321,18.
15. 1,321,24.
16. 1,320,25 *jucunda*.
17. 1,320,3 movent. 320,22 provocent.
18. 1,321,32.
19. 1,322,9.
20. 1,322,12.
21. 1,323,3.
22. 1,323,27.
23. 1,319,30.
24. See J. Wicks, *Man Yearning for Grace*, Chapter II, Section 4; Chapter IV, Section 8; and Chapter 5, Seciton 4, Sub-section *iii*.
25. Wicks, *op.cit.*, 70ff. See also the passages referred to in the previous note.
26. 1,321,20.
27. 2,720,5-7.
28. 2,719,35.
29. 2,722,7.
30. 6,548,20.
31. 2,715,30.
32. 2,714,17; 721,10.
33. 2,716,18.
34. 2,715,28.
35. 2,719,8.
36. 2,716,27.
37. 2,721,1.

38. 2,720,21f.
39. 2,722,30.
40. 2,728,8.
41. 2,729,34.
42. 2,730,30ff.
43. 2,733,39.
44. 2,732,3.
45. 6,534,15.
46. 6,532,24.
47. 6,533,33.
48. 6,538,17.
49. 6,532,27.
50. 6,533,15.
51. 6,532f.
52. 6,545,1.
53. 6,572,15.
54. 6,546,11.
55. 6,543,31.
56. 6,528,4.
57. 6,527,37.
58. 2,722,3.
59. 6,531,8.
60. 6,529,36.
61. 6,528,20.
62. 2,730,30.
63. 2,733,16.
64. 6,529,13.
65. 6,533,32.
66. 6,359,6.
67. 2,749,35.
68. 2,750,4.
69. 2,743,7. The following two quotations are from 2,748,8 and 748,34.
70. In German the word f o r "body" (*Leib*) and the ancient word for "loaf" (*Laib*) are homonyms, indistinguishable in Luther's spelling.
71. Althaus, *op.cit.*, p.275, footnote 110, pp.277f, and 320. Cf. WA 6,131,37.
72. 25,137,31; 31II,118,30.
73. 6,354,18.
74. 6,355,34; 512,33; 515,17.
75. 6,513,32.

76. 6,514,21.
77. 6,516,30.
78. 6,515,22; 518,10.
79. 6,363,6; 373,32; 10II,29,18.
80. 6,518,20.
81. 6,358,14.
82. 6,519,34; 361,5.
83. 6,362,6.
84. 6,515,27.
85. 6,368,5.
86. 6,360,21.
87. 30I,226,24 and 230,29.
88. 6,365,6.
89. 6,516,5. Cf.6,517,37: "ipsa verba sedula et plena fide meditentur."
90. Althaus, *op.cit.*, 338.
91. 6,368,12.
92. Althaus, *op.cit.*, 278 and 320.
93. Other examples are found in Luther's *Auslegung deutsch des Vater Unser* (WA 2), in his *Small Commentary on Galatians* (WA 2), in his *Sermon von dem hl. hochw. Sacrament der Taufe* (WA 2), in his *Sermon von der Bereitung zum Sterben* (WA 2), and in *Tessaradecas* (WA 6). All these writings were composed or re-edited in 1519.
94. For example: *De votis monasticis* (WA 8), *An den christlichen Adel* (WA 6), *Dass eine christliche Gemeine Macht und Recht habe . . .* (WA 11).
95. 8,pp.606ff.
96. 8,pp.613 and 683f.
97. 6,560,33.
98. For instance, 25,16,17.
99. For instance, 38,pp.229f.
100. 6,564,11; 566,26; 25,16,23; 38, 230,21; 49,600,11, and many other passages.
101. 6,407,22; 564,6 and many other passages.

102. 6,370,8.
103. 6,412f.
104. 38,214,2.
105. 6,301,3 and 7,20,34.

106. 6,412,20; 12,188,15, and other passages.
107. 25,27,31; 40I,63,30.
108. 18,653,22; 609,5.

NOTES TO CHAPTER VI

1. 5,248,29; 7, p.222ff.
2. 2,490,13.
3. 2,113f.
4. 8,684,27.
5. 5,166,25; 167,12.
6. 1,540,33.38; 5,167,11.
7. For example, 40III,637,16.
8. 5,385,2.
9. 5,387,5. Luther sets forth his view as a commentary on Ps. 12/13:1-3.
10. 1,540,8.
11. 7,227f.
12. Cf. also 7,223,2.
13. 40II,12,5; cf. 40I,580,14.
14. Ebeling, *Das Wesen des christlichen Glaubens* (Siebenstern ed.), pp.156-158 and 173.
15. 5,248,30; 385,26; 7,227,15; 40I, 12,3.
16. 56,204,23.
17. 40I,pp.581ff.
18. 40I,88,1; 89,1.
19. For characteristic examples of exterior defiance see 12,217,17 and 18,107,27.
20. 46,106,16.
21. 10III,350,31.
22. 31II,3,5; cf. 40I,223,9.29.
23. 6,519,34 and 520,4.
24. 40I,578,22.
25. 40I,372,21.
26. See, for example, 31I,pp.166-171.
27. An example as late as 1519 is 2,526,22.
28. Ebeling, *Das Wesen des christlichen Glaubens,* 156.
29. 4,647,29.
30. 56,387,4.
31. 4,pp.645-648.
32. 40I,pp.76f.
33. 40I,pp.78-81.
34. *Contra Haereses* IV,20,5.
35. 6,360,21. See above Chapter V, Section 4.
36. *Luther, Einführung in sein Denken.* Ebeling describes his introduction as a "traveling along the great antitheses in Luther's thinking" (p. 179). Ten of the fourteen chapters of Ebeling's book deal with antitheses: philosophy and theology, letter and spirit, law and gospel, the twofold use of the law, person and work, faith and love, Christ's realm and the realm of the world, Christian person and secular person, freedom and bondage, the hidden God and the manifest God.
37. *Das Wesen des christlichen Glaubens.*
38. 56,229,7.
39. 5,161,16.18.
40. 5,195,41.
41. 6,529,11.
42. 6,527,38.
43. 40I,90,12.
44. WBr 2, no.424; p.372,83.
45. WBr 5, no.1670; p.520,64.
46. 40II,342,16.
47. 5,248,12.